Unusual Prophecies Being Fulfilled

PROPHETIC SERIES | BOOK SEVEN

UNDERSTANDING *the* PROPHETIC TIMES *and* SEASONS WE ARE IN

Unusual Prophecies Being Fulfilled

2015 *and* Beyond:
Cosmic Prophecies *for the* Last Days

PERRY STONE

UNUSUAL PROPHECIES BEING FULFILLED
Published by Voice of Evangelism Ministries
P. O. Box 3595
Cleveland, Tennessee 37320

No part of this book may be reproduced in any form, stored in a retrieval system, or transmitted in any form by any means—electronic, mechanical, photocopy, recording, or otherwise—without prior written permission of the publisher, except as provided by United States of America copyright law.

Unless otherwise noted, all Scripture quotations are from the King James Version of the Bible.

Copyright © 2009 by Voice of Evangelism, Inc.
All rights reserved.

ISBN 0-9785920-9-3

Printed in the United States of America

This book is the seventh in a series written by Perry Stone under the title, *Unusual Prophecies Being Fulfilled*. Other books are:

Book 1: Unusual Prophecies: Tsunamis, Volcanoes, and Earthquakes in Prophecy
Book 2: Unusual Prophecies: Islamic Prophecies and Terrorism Against America
Book 3: Unusual Prophecies: America's Amazing Prophetic Cycles and Patterns
Book 4: Unusual Prophecies: The Pope, the Eagle, and the Iron Sickle
Book 5: Unusual Prophecies: Jerusalem's Mysterious Connection to the Garden of Eden
Book 6: Unusual Prophecies: Prophecies Being Fulfilled Inside Israel

The International Offices of the Voice of Evangelism
P. O. Box 3595
Cleveland, Tennessee 37320
(423) 478-3456
www.voe.org

Contents

	Dedication	7
	Introduction	9
Chapter 1	The End of the Age—Again and Again and Again	11
Chapter 2	From Egypt to Rome: How Ancient People Viewed Cosmic Avtivity	27
Chapter 3	Prophecies Among the Ancient Indians	47
Chapter 4	Cosmic Signs Linked to Israel and the Year 2015	55
Chapter 5	Living During the Birth Pains of the Messiah	63
Chapter 6	The Sign of the Son of Man in Heaven	79
Chapter 7	The Sign of the Coming of the Son of Man	97
Chapter 8	Great and Fearful Signs From the Second Heaven	109
Chapter 9	Preparing for the Final Redemption	117

Dedication

With great love and appreciation, I wish to dedicate this book, number seven in the prophetic series, to my beloved father, Perry Fred Stone, Sr., whose prayer life, integrity, and love for God served as an example to me and all who met him. He taught me a love for the Word of God that remained and has continued to increase. After preaching the gospel for over fifty-eight years, he once said, "I always believed in the return of Christ; but son, your generation is seeing the signs fulfilled that my generation never saw."

Dad, you are my mentor and my hero. I love you.

Introduction

People have been interested in the timing of Christ's return since the day He ascended back to Heaven around the year 32 AD. Anticipation was high in the early church, because many believed He would return in the first century, especially before the death of John, the beloved disciple and revelator. Throughout history, believers have watched for the signs of Christ's return. Many leaders who persecuted Christians and were responsible for wars and social turmoil were believed to be the antichrist. But all of those men eventually died, and the alleged signs of Christ's soon return came and went as life on earth continued.

Today, modern events—for example, wars in the Middle East—are often viewed as an indication of the soon return of Christ. Again, these events happen and then come to an end; but the church is still here and life goes on. I refer to these kinds of events as prophetic steppingstones, not prophetic milestones. A milestone is an event that is specifically predicted in Scripture—for example, Israel becoming a nation in 1948. A steppingstone is an event that is not a direct fulfillment of biblical prophecy, but which can and will eventually lead to the fulfillment of prophecies. The war in Iraq is one example of a steppingstone.

Christ told us that one sign of the end of the age would be signs in the heavens. Throughout history, there have been strange cosmic occurrences that preceded major biblical events. There was even unusual cosmic activity at the birth of Christ, which led the wise me to say, "We have seen His star in the east." What was that cosmic sign? What was the star of the Jewish King? How did the ancient astrologers and oracles know what was soon to happen, based on the signs in the heavens?

The secular media has been telling us that the world could end in 2012. What is the significance of the year 2012? What did the prophet Joel mean when he prophesied that the sun would be darkened and the moon turn to blood before the great and terrible day of the Lord? How are those events linked to the nation of Israel? What does the Bible refer to when it tells us that there will be shaking in the heavens?

Christ warned that, before His return, there would be famines, earthquakes, and pestilences, as well as fearful and great signs from the heavens. Because of the scientific technology that is available today, we are now able to explain cosmic signs that were described by biblical prophets thousands of years ago.

In the chapters that follow, we will examine the signs that have occurred throughout history, as well as the signs that we are seeing today and those that are expected in the future. In our modern era, we now can understand the heavenly signs of the final generation!

CHAPTER 1

The End of the Age— Again and Again and Again

"Now as He sat on the Mount of Olives, the disciples came to Him privately, saying, "Tell us, when will these things be? And what will be the sign of Your coming, and of the end of the age?"

–Matthew 24:3

It was the late sixteenth century, and along the rivers and lakes in Austria, Germany people were building arks. They were mostly simple farmers using hammers, nails, and hewn trees to build large boats that would protect their families from another global flood, similar to the flood of Noah's day. The people were following the prophetic instructions of an astrologer and self-acclaimed prophet, Johann Stoffler. According to the allegedly irrefutable calculations of Stoffler, another massive flood was about to strike all of Europe, and the only survivors of this deadly deluge would be those who followed his instruction to prepare arks for the saving of their families.

The date came and went without any storms, floods, or destruction. In retrospect, if the people had possessed Bibles and could have read

God's promise to Noah, every time they saw a rainbow draping the sky they would have known that God made a covenant to never again destroy the earth by water (Genesis 9:13-16). Another astronomer entered the scene—another alleged prophet from Vienna, Austria named Georg Tannenstetter. He disproved the calculation of Stoffler and declared that no flood would come. Oh well, so much for the houseboats. (source: *The Story of Prophecy*, Henry Forman, Tudor Publishing Co., NY, 1940. Chapter VI, pages 97-98)

Since the ascension of Christ in or around 32 AD, history has been replete with these types of stories. A person calculates a date, makes a prediction of the timing of a Biblical revelation, stirs peoples' concern, and the date passes and life goes on. The Bible does use certain timeframes in selective prophetic passages, and often these timeframes have been used to calculate dates for the rise of the Antichrist, the tribulation, and the second coming of Christ.

Other dates, such as 1260 and 1290, are believed to be the inspiration for the infamous crusades that continued from 1095 to 1291. The Pope called for Christians to take back the Holy Land from the grip of the Muslims, and the result was a war that became known as the crusades. A total of ten crusades ensued over a two-hundred-year period. The timing for these war-like efforts was prophetically significant and based on the timeframes of 1260 and 1290 from the book of Daniel (Daniel 12:7, 11-12). Since the years 1260 and 1290 AD would approach in the future, it appeared that God would favor the zealous Christians for delivering the land of God from the hands of the Muslims. It was clear that the predictions failed when the Muslims re-captured the Holy Land in 1291, bringing a conclusion to the crusades.

In more contemporary times, who can forget the small booklet, *88 Reasons why Jesus will Return in 1988*, or the Y2K computer scare that swept the world as people stockpiled food and survival items, only to have enough batteries and beans to last for months or even years.

Ever since the ascension of Christ in or around the year 32 AD, there has been an interest in the very last promise made as Christ ascended back to the heavenly Temple to serve as Heaven's High Priest (Hebrews 4:14-16). The final prophecy was announced by two men in white clothes who promised:

> *"Now when He had spoken these things, while they watched, He was taken up, and a cloud received Him out of their sight. And while they looked steadfastly toward heaven as He went up, behold, two men stood by them in white apparel, who also said, "Men of Galilee, why do you stand gazing up into heaven? This same Jesus, who was taken up from you into heaven, will so come in like manner as you saw Him go into heaven."* —Acts 1:9-11

From that moment, believers have anticipated the return of Christ. Years later the Apostle Paul revealed the manner of Christ's return for the church and the resurrection of the dead in Christ:

> *"For this we say to you by the word of the Lord, that we who are alive and remain until the coming of the Lord will by no means precede those who are asleep. For the Lord Himself will descend from heaven with a shout, with the voice of an archangel, and with the trumpet of God. And the dead in Christ will rise first. Then we who are alive and remain shall be caught up together with them in the*

clouds to meet the Lord in the air. And thus we shall always be with the Lord. Therefore comfort one another with these words."

–1 Thessalonians 4:15-18

Once the promise of Christ's return spread throughout the early church, there was high anticipation that Christ could return in the first century. Paul said, "We who are alive and remain…so shall we ever be with the Lord." The use of the pronoun *we* indicated that Paul was referring to himself and those living in his day. Did Paul actually believe that Christ *could* return in his day? Apparently there was a belief circulating that, not only could Christ return in the first century, but that one apostle, namely John, would still be alive at the return of the Messiah.

The Man Who Saw the Future

After Christ's resurrection He met with His eleven disciples at the Sea of Galilee for a fish fry. Peter asked Jesus questions, and Jesus predicted that Peter would live to be an old man (John 21:18-19). Peter turned to the Apostle John, the youngest of the disciples and said, "What about this man?" Christ answered, *"If I want him to stay (survive, live) until I come, what is that to you? [What concern is it of yours?]* – (John 21:22 – AMP). From that moment a rumor began spreading far and wide in the early church that John would be alive at the return of the Lord: *"Then this saying went out among the brethren that this disciple would not die. Yet Jesus did not say to him that he would not die, but, "If I will that he remain till I come, what is that to you?"* – John 21:23

Jesus already had told his followers, *"Assuredly, I say to you, there are some standing here who shall not taste death till they see the Son of*

Man coming in His kingdom" (Matthew 16:28). From that moment, the disciples began to anticipate the setting up of the kingdom of the Messiah on earth during their generation, and they linked John's length of life to a sign of Christ's return. This is why, prior to Christ's ascension into heaven, the disciples were anticipating the setting up of the kingdom on earth. They asked:

> *"Therefore, when they had come together, they asked Him, saying, "Lord, will You at this time restore the kingdom to Israel?" And He said to them, "It is not for you to know times or seasons which the Father has put in His own authority."* —Acts 1:6-7

Moments later, when Christ was ascending, His followers were gazing into heaven, perhaps anticipating that Christ would ascend, then immediately return to set up the kingdom. After all, they were standing on the Mount of Olives, the very mountain upon which the prophet Zechariah predicted that Christ would one day return and set his feet upon, causing the mountain to split in half (Zechariah 14:1-4). Christ did not return that day, but the disciples were immediately informed that He would return in the same manner that He went up.

Except for John, all of the original apostles eventually were martyred. *The Foxes Book of Martyrs* reveals the manner in which they died. Phillip traveled to upper Asia where he was scourged and crucified. Matthias, the apostle selected to replace Judas (Acts 1:23-26), was stoned in Jerusalem and beheaded. Andrew went to Edessa and later faced death by crucifixion. Bartholomew translated Matthew's gospel in India and was later beaten and crucified. Thomas also became an evangelist to India where, according to the Christians in India, he performed many miracles as a sign of Christ's power. Later Thomas was thrust through with a spear. History tells us that Peter was crucified upside down because he felt he was not worthy to be crucified in the same manner of his Lord. The only apostle of the original group that was still living after all others were martyred was John.

In the year 70 AD, when the Temple was burned, Jerusalem destroyed, and the Jewish people scattered or taken as slaves, there was high anticipation that Christ would certainly be returning. After all, John was still living; in fact, he lived another twenty-five years. Instead of John living to see the *physical* return of Christ, he saw the kingdom when he experienced the vision called the apocalypse while a prisoner on the Island of Patmos! John lived to write about the heavenly Temple, the seven-sealed book, the four horsemen of the apocalypse, the Marriage Supper of the Lamb, and the return of the King to rule for one thousand years. No other prophet or apostle had ever seen or described the city of the New Jerusalem as John did. Indeed, he did not die until he saw the Son of Man coming in the kingdom and recorded the future events in Revelation chapters 4 through 22! Thus the words of Jesus were fulfilled through John, but in a manner the disciples would not have expected.

Theology Changed After John's Death

When John died and Christ did not return by the year 100 AD, the Christian fathers then began to believe that they were nearing the time of the revealing of the antichrist and the tribulation. The emperor Nero had burnt Rome and blamed it on the Christians, resulting in the beheading of Paul in Rome. Starting with Nero's persecution of the saints in and around Rome, the church would experience ten persecutions by Roman emperors. Once again, *The Foxes Book of Martyrs* lists the ten primitive persecutions that befell the church in the first three centuries:

- Nero   AD 67
- Domitian   AD 81
- Trajan   AD 108
- Antoninus   AD 162
- Severus   AD 192
- Maximux   AD 235
- Decius   AD 249
- Valerian   AD 257
- Aurelian   AD 274
- Diocletian   AD 303

A New Date is Set

After these persecutions, the Emperor Constantine, the first to accept Christianity, took the Imperial Roman throne (312 to 337) and endorsed Christianity. From then onward, the theology of the church began to change. Many began to believe that the church would initiate a one thousand year reign of Christ on earth, with the leaders of the Christian (especially the Roman) church setting up their own kings and rulers throughout Europe. The two main religious groups were the Roman Catholics, with their Popes that ruled the western branch from Rome, Italy, and the eastern branch of Byzantine Christians (the Byzantine Empire) that set up its headquarters in Constantinople, Turkey.

Several post-Nicaea fathers, using the Septuagint calculation of Biblical time (which was off by fifteen hundred years), taught that from Adam to the 5th century was a full six thousand years, and that the Kingdom of the Messiah would come to earth by the 5th century. As the time approached, the prophecies were revised. Instead of a literal return of Christ to rule for one thousand years, a doctrine emerged that said the church, rather than Christ Himself, would set up the one-thousand-year reign of Christ through the Popes (called the Vicar of Christ). From the 5th century onward, only during certain timeframes was there a surge of interest in the return of Christ.

From time to time, self-acclaimed prophets would research the Scriptures and come up with prophetic dates upon which they were certain Christ would return. From the 2nd to the 5th century, the arrival of the dreaded antichrist was a central theme among many bishops in the church. St. Martin, Bishop of Tours, made a stunning prediction in 380 AD that the antichrist was a small lad living on earth. Years passed without his appearing. Another announcement came around 1080, when the Bishop of Florence said the antichrist was born and the end of the age was near.

Several of the Biblical numbers that peak interest in apocalyptic literature were interpreted, not by Biblical prophets, but by students and some scholars of Scripture, as prophetic *years*. The following numbers became years, and key events were believed to be linked to these years. Following are some examples:

Number	Scripture Reference	Interpretation
666	Revelation 13:18	the year 666
1000	Revelation 20:2	the year 1000
1260	Revelation 11:3	the year 1260
1290	Daniel 12:11	the year 1290
1335	Daniel 12:12	the year 1335
2000	Hosea 6:2	the year 2000

As one example, in the year 989 AD, a Monk wrote that Satan would be loosed on the earth in the year 1000. He based this on one reference in Revelation that says, "Satan will be loosed for one thousand years" (Revelation 20:7). He predicted that a terrible time was coming to earth and that believers should prepare. Fuel was added to the fire when, several years before the year 1000, a large comet—now identified as Haley's Comet—passed through the galaxy.

In the year 999 there was high anticipation that Christ would return to Jerusalem. Many Christians were motivated to sell their property and homes, don white robes, and make the long pilgrimage from nations in Europe to the Holy City of Jerusalem. Among the multitudes making the trek were knights, citizens, serfs, and their families, who came worshipping, singing, and arriving with palm branches in their hands as they looked upward for the arrival of the Messiah. So many made the journey that they were compared to a desolating army. Many of the buildings in the Holy Land fell into ruin, since the people did not want to spend money on repairs or the pruning of vines when the end of the age was near. When the year 1000 passed and neither Jesus nor Satan appeared, the believers went on with life.

A second wave of interest swept the land when a group called the Lombards linked the Vikings and their dragon ships with the dragon Satan that would rise up out of the sea (Revelation 12:9 and 13:1-2). They began to identify the Vikings with the antichrist because, since Christ was crucified around 32 to 33 AD, the year 1033 would be one thousand years since the event. The Bible mentions "ruling and reigning with Christ for a thousand years" (Revelation 20:6); thus, the Lombards calculated that the Lord should return to earth on the year 1033. If the Vikings were ushering in the antichrist and the dates were correct, then the time of the end was near.

Their predictions spread like wildfire and, as the date approached, believers sold their possessions and made pilgrimage to the city in which they knew Christ would return—Jerusalem. But the date passed and believers returned to business as usual as they continued the work of the church.

The books of Daniel and Revelation reveal several important timeframes in ancient prophecy. They are 1,260 days (Revelation 11:3), 1,290 days (Daniel 12:11), and 1,335 days (Daniel 12:12). Both Daniel and John reveal these timeframes as days and not years. However, there is a spiritual principle in the Bible where God changes days into years. When Moses sent men from each tribe to spy out the Promised Land, all except Caleb and Joshua returned and expressed unbelief, causing the Israelites to doubt God's promises. Their punishment was to wander in the wilderness for forty years, a year for each day they spent spying out the land (Numbers 14:34).

Using the day for a year theory, some scholars began to teach that major prophetic events would transpire on the years 1260, 1290, or 1335.

Dating from the birth of Christ, the 13th century was expected to be a major timeframe for prophetic events, even possibly the return of Christ. During this time, battles were breaking out between Muslims and European Christians.

The Crusaders and the Muslims

In the 7th century the Muslims took over Palestine and Jerusalem, building a mosque on the Temple Mount platform where two previous Jewish Temples had once stood. Eventually the Popes and other religious leaders initiated a war against the Muslims to retake the Holy Land and Jerusalem from the possession of the Muslims. The European Christians who fought these wars were known as Crusaders. The first crusade was fought when Byzantine emperor Alexios I requested that Pope Urban II provide mercenaries to help fight the Muslim advance toward land controlled by the Byzantines. The first Crusade occurred in 1095. There were nine crusades from the 11th to 13th centuries, all during the timeframes that were prophetically significant: 1260 to 1290.

During the early 13th century, an alleged prophet named Joachim claimed to have received a divine visitation in which it was revealed to him that the antichrist would soon arise and take the throne of the Pope. In his writings, Joachim predicted three great epochs, all linked to the three prophetic dates mentioned in the apocalypse. The first epoch linked to God the Father was the present Christian era (the 12th century). The second epoch, in which Jesus the Son would dominate, was supposed to climax in the year 1260 AD. The third epoch was to begin in the year 1260 and was to be manifested by the Holy Ghost, in which He would initiate a complete cleansing of the church. The next timeframe that

Joachim was examining was the year 1335, but he died in 1202.

Not all predictions were inaccurate. In the 4th century Methodius, Bishop of Patara, predicted that the Ishmaelites (Arabs) would conquer and dominate many Christian lands as God's punishment for the sins of the members and ministers in the church. Hundreds of years later, Mohammad arose in Arabia and initiated a new religion called Islam. True to the Bishop's prophecy, Mohammad's Arab followers began marching into lands once controlled by Christians. (source: *The Story of Prophecy*, Henry Forman, C. 1940, Tudor Publishing Company, New York, pages 98, 104-105).

Six centuries before it occurred, the Emperor Leo (886-889) foretold that the city of Constantinople, the headquarters of Byzantine Christianity, would be overrun by Muslims who would conquer the city. In a series of tablets later discovered in Constantinople, Leo revealed, in succession, the actual names of the emperors and patriarchs for the next six hundred years. On the tablets every name had its space, but the last space was empty, revealing the timeframe when the prediction would occur. Eventually, the Muslim Turks did invade the city of Byzantium, killing an emperor named Constantine, the last man predicted to be the final Byzantine emperor.

The End of the Age—Again and Again

If you think that prophetic preaching and emphasis on the time of the end and the return of the Messiah has been revived only in the 20th century as some allege, then the list below will dispel that myth. This list reveals the person making the prediction of Christ's return, the time the prediction was made, and the expected time of fulfillment.

The Person(s)	Date of Prediction	Expected Fulfillment
Mantanu	156 AD	Near Future
Prisca & Maximilla	156 AD	Near Future
Novatian	4th century	Near Future
Donatus	4th century	Near Future
John of Toeldo	1186	Near Future
Melchior Hofmann	153	1531
Sabbati Zevi	1647	1666
Johann Zimmerman	1693	1694
George Rapp	1804	Near Future
William Miller	1839	1843
Henry Adams	1903	1950
Alexander Bedward	1920	December 31, 1920
Herbert Armstrong	1934	1972, 1976
John Strong	1977	October, 1978
Edgar Wisenutt	1987	1988, 1989
Jehovah's Witnesses	Various Dates	1914, 1976, etc.

Even though people have predicted the date of Christ's return since He ascended to Heaven, an emphasis on His return has increased since the restoration of Israel as a nation in 1948. However, the rebirth of Israel was not based upon the speculation of self-appointed prophets; instead, it was predicted by inspired prophets in the Holy Bible.

Modern Predictions that Missed Their Target

In my own lifetime I have spent many thousands of hours in personal study and research of the Bible, Jewish history, and prophetic themes.

Over the years, I have observed that certain events would trigger prophetic interest among Christians, and at times even among non-believers. Four of those events have occurred since 1991.

The first was the 1991 Gulf War, which united a thirty-four nation coalition against Iraq for invading neighboring Kuwait. The United States and Great Britain led the coalition to expel Iraqi forces from Kuwait. On January 17, 1991, when the war was initiated with an air campaign to destroy Iraqi radar systems, I was ministering at Church of the Harvest in Cleveland, Tennessee. As news broke that America was now at war in the Middle East, the church filled to capacity with people sitting in the lobby and others trying to get inside. People were willing to stand outdoors in cold weather with the doors open, just to hear a prophetic update.

There was great concern that the oldest nation (Iraq, formerly known as Babylon) was battling the world's youngest empire (America), and that the battle would spread into neighboring Islamic nations to create the scenario for the Gog and Magog conflict. Even some journalists were calling this "the mother of all battles that could lead to Armageddon." Forty days later the war was over and neither Gog and Magog nor Armageddon had occurred. Things eventually went back to normal in America.

Prophetic speculation increased again prior to Y2K, or the potential computer fiasco that was expected to occur as the year 1999 rolled over to the year 2000. The theory was that computers and internal clocks in certain electronic devices could not accurately read the date when the clocks rolled to the year 2000. Computer specialists appeared on national news programs and painted doom and gloom scenarios of computer failures, power grid shutdowns, non-functioning gas pumps, and bank failures. Survival stores prospered and huge spikes in food purchases occurred globally. Everyone felt great relief when the New Year arrived and we experienced only minor computer glitches.

The third event to bring prophetic speculation was the September 11, 2001 attack on America. During the seven remaining years of George W. Bush's presidency, America did not experience another attack on her soil, although a former U.S. Congressman informed me that about thirty-five planned attacks were stopped due to the vigilance of Homeland Security and other government agencies, local citizens, and agencies in other countries. The September 11 attacks caused fear in the hearts of many people—not just because of the shocking new reports, but because of the potential for future terrorist attacks.

When deadly anthrax was mailed on September 18, 2001 to news agencies and two U.S. Senators, fear intensified. Twenty-two people developed anthrax infections and five eventually died. Would this conflict thrust America into an all-out war against Islam? Were thousands of terrorists lurking in the shadows, waiting for a cryptic signal to make their move, killing thousands of Americans with anthrax or some unknown weapon of mass destruction? A few years passed and the fear of terrorism subsided. Eventually, the 44th president announced that he would close the Guantanamo Bay Detention Facility where suspected terrorists were being held and bring the detainees to America. When President George W. Bush directed troops into Afghanistan and later Iraq, once again there was a rise in prophetic fever. For years the United States government had evidence that Saddam Hussein possessed an arsenal of chemical and biological weapons that could fall into the hands of terrorists. In his book, *Saddam's Secrets,* former Iraqi General George Sada stated that, before the Iraqi war, Saddam's dangerous weapons and chemical agents were transported to Syria on fifty-six flights via Iraqi jets that had the seats removed. Some military sources say that the intelligence was flawed and there were no weapons of mass destruction in Iraq, even though Saddam had used them on his own people when he gassed and killed many of the Kurds.

I call these events prophetic *steppingstones,* not *milestones.* A prophetic milestone is an event that is specifically predicted by the prophets, Christ, or the New Testament apostles. A milestone clearly predicts an event that comes to pass, even giving minute details. A steppingstone is not a direct fulfillment of Biblical prophecy, but it is an event that can and will eventually lead to major prophetic scenarios and fulfillment.

The 2012 Predictions

Another event predicted by secular prognosticators is a series of fearful cosmic events that will, according to the ancient Mayan Indian calendar, occur in December 2012. Is this another one of those hyped-up predictions that will produce nothing but more skepticism of prophecies? Or is there a mystery that the Mayan's knew that has resurfaced in our generation? Before exploring the prediction of 2012, let's examine some lesser known historical events and see how the ancient people of Greece and Rome looked toward the heavens and linked cosmic activity to their own destinies.

CHAPTER 2

From Egypt to Rome: How Ancient People Viewed Cosmic Activity

"As for these four children, God gave them knowledge and skill in all learning and wisdom: and Daniel had understanding in all visions and dreams. Now at the end of the days that the king had said he should bring them in, then the prince of the eunuchs brought them in before Nebuchadnezzar.

"And the king communed with them; and among them all was found none like Daniel, Hananiah, Mishael, and Azariah: therefore stood they before the king. And in all matters of wisdom and understanding, that the king inquired of them, he found them ten times better than all the magicians and astrologers that were in all his realm." —Daniel 1:17-20 (KJV)

The above Scripture is speaking of young Hebrew men who were taken captive to ancient Babylon in the days of King Nebuchadnezzar. Ancient empires such as Egypt, Babylon, Greece, and Rome were very familiar with the cosmos and the positioning of the sun, moon, and stars. Each empire had "wise men" whose assignment was to interpret the times by observing the position of certain stars, eclipses, and comets. Such was the case in ancient Babylon, where Daniel and these other young men lived during the seventy-year captivity of the Hebrew people (Jeremiah 25:11).

The book of Daniel contains twelve chapters. There are numerous spiritual dreams and visions recorded throughout the book, most relating to future prophetic events and empires and their impact on Israel and the Jews. For example, Daniel chapter two records King Nebuchadnezzar's dream of the metallic image; chapter four tells the king's dream of the tree with the iron band; the handwriting on the wall is mentioned in chapter five; and chapters seven and eight give the visions of the beast.

Normally, the king would appeal to his wise men and astrologers to interpret the dreams. In each case, the King of Babylon sought out the expertise of his cosmic committee; but in each situation, all failed to interpret Nebuchadnezzar's troubling dreams. In chapters two, four, and five, we see that it was Daniel who received the divine inspiration to interpret the king's nightmares. Daniel said:

> "...The [mysterious] secret which the king has demanded neither the wise men, enchanters, magicians, nor astrologers can show the king." –Daniel 2:27 (AMP)

The Spirit of the Lord that rested upon Daniel, and a special gift that God had imparted to his life, enabled him to understand these mysteries.

The same was true with Joseph. No wise men or astrologer could understand the dream of Pharaoh; but Joseph received the divine interpretation, warned the leader of a seven-year famine, and then revealed the solution for survival (Genesis 41).

In ancient times, a man who was gifted at seeing into the future or interpreting dreams was called a seer, because he could see into the future or foretell events. Being a seer was a dangerous job; for example:

- If they told the king something good, they could live;
- If they told him something bad, they could be killed;
- If they saw bad and predicted good, they were slain.

One example is found in 2 Chronicles 18. Four hundred "prophets" told King Ahab that, if he engaged in a battle, he would be victorious. His coalition partner, Jehoshaphat, asked for a second opinion from a prophet of God. The real prophet—the prophet of God—was dragged out of a dungeon and informed on his way to the palace that he should predict only good to Ahab. This prophet, Micaiah, tickled the king's ears and said, "Go and prosper and you will win" (2 Chronicles 18:14). After a rebuke Ahab said, "Give me the real word of the Lord!" The prophet replied, "You asked for it and here it is!" Micaiah then predicted the death of the king (2 Chronicles 18:21).

Immediately there was a stirring among the four hundred "yes men" who had predicted the opposite. Somebody was wrong and heads were going to roll. Micaiah warned one of the false prophets that he would end up hiding in fear when the king was killed in battle (2 Chronicles 18:24). Of course the prophet from the dungeon was right. The reason he was living in the basement was because he was always giving a negative word to the king (2 Chronicles 18:17).

From a Biblical perspective, the only men who could accurately discern the times were men in whom the Spirit of the Living God dwelt. All others were hit-and-miss.

Three Puzzling Dreams

One of the interesting mysteries related to world leaders and spiritual dreams is the fact that three of the most important dreams recorded in Scripture were given to men who were not believers in the true God. Pharaoh, Nebuchadnezzar, and the Magi who traveled to Bethlehem were all worshippers of other gods, but were directly influenced by the men of God (Joseph and Daniel, for example). Nebuchadnezzar eventually converted to the Hebrew God (Daniel chapter 5).

If God reveals visions and dreams through His Spirit, then why did He speak to two kings who no doubt worshipped idols, giving them two of the most amazing prophetic dreams in the Bible? I believe there are three answers:

1. These were men of influence who had large followings. Had a simple man received the revelation, no one would have believed it or acted upon it. The fact that they were known and respected gave credence to the dreams.

2. God exalted His name and His men (Joseph and Daniel) into the highest positions of the kingdom through their ability to interpret the dreams of the kings. Thus, there was a heavenly ulterior motive for giving the kings the dreams—to exalt God's men into high government positions at the right time.

3. The dreams gave the leaders an opportunity to believe in the only true God who was able to predict the future with accuracy, thus turning them away from their useless idols and their inaccurate, sign-seeking wise men.

Each of the three—Pharaoh, Nebuchadnezzar and the Magi—had a predestined prophetic assignment that was fulfilled without their prior knowledge. Pharaoh allowed the Hebrews to live in Egypt because of Joseph's wisdom, while Nebuchadnezzar brought Israel into captivity to fulfill a prophecy from Jeremiah. The Magi provided gold, frankincense, and myrrh to the Christ child. These special items could be sold and the income used as financial provision for the family's journey to Egypt.

Review of Ancient Predictions

Ancient predictions date back as far as the first man, Adam. Josephus wrote about the sons of Adam, namely Seth, and their discoveries:

"They also were the inventors of that peculiar sort of wisdom which is concerned with the heavenly bodies and their order. And that their inventions might not be lost before they were sufficiently known, upon Adam's prediction that the world was to be destroyed at one time by the force of fire and another time by the violence and quantity of water, they made two pillars; the one of brick, and the other of stone: they inscribed their discoveries on them both, that in case the pillar of brick should be destroyed by the flood, the pillar of stone might remain, and exhibit those discoveries to mankind; and also inform them that there was another pillar of brick erected by them. Now this remains in the land of Siriad to this day." — *Josephus, Antiquities of the Jews*, Chapter II, part 3

Adam was told that two forms of judgment would occur on the earth. One was a watery judgment which occurred 1,658 years after Adam through Noah's flood; the other was a future prediction that the world will be destroyed by fire. This is also written in the book of 2 Peter 3:7.

The second historical reference to a person receiving revelations from God is the seventh man from Adam—a man named Enoch. There is a non-canonical book of Enoch, although the Ethiopian Orthodox Church teaches that it is canonical. The book was known and even quoted by some fathers in the early church. The book of Enoch is quoted in Jude 1:14-15 and is also referenced in the Dead Sea Scrolls that were written by the Qumran community. Some church fathers suggested it was rejected by the Jews because it contained prophecies concerning Christ.

The book of Enoch is divided into five sections:

- the book of the watchers
- the book of parables of Enoch
- the astronomical book
- the book of dreams and visions
- the epistle of Enoch

The Biblical quote that references the prophecy of Enoch says:

"Now Enoch, the seventh from Adam, prophesied about these men also, saying, "Behold, the Lord comes with ten thousands of His saints,

to execute judgment on all, to convict all who are ungodly among them of all their ungodly deeds which they have committed in an ungodly way, and of all the harsh things which ungodly sinners have spoken against Him." —Jude 1:14-15

The quote from the book of Enoch, rediscovered in 1773, says it this way: "And behold, he comes with myriads of the holy to pass judgment upon them, and will destroy the impious, and will call to account all flesh for everything the sinners and the impious have done and committed against him" (Enoch 1:9).

Recall that Enoch, at age sixty-five, began walking with God and was translated without seeing death at 365 years of age (Genesis 5:24). Enoch had a son named Methuselah, whose Hebrew name means, "his death brings, or his death initiates." Oddly, Methuselah lived to be 969 years of age and died the same year of the flood. He was a sign to those living in his day that, when he died, the predicted destruction of the earth would come. Thus, Enoch was the first man to predict the coming of the Lord to rule with His saints!

Ancient Signs of Noble Births

Several scrolls (books) that existed in the time of David and Solomon no longer exist or have yet to be discovered. These include the book of Gad (1 Chronicles 29:29), the book of Nathan the prophet (1 Chronicles 29:29), and the book of the Wars of the Lord (Numbers 21:14). Another book mentioned in Joshua 10:13 and 2 Samuel 1:18 is the book of Jasher. In the 1800s, a book called the book of Jasher was found and translated from Hebrew to English. It is not inspired as Scripture, but it is considered sacred history and often gives details that fill in the blanks of many Biblical stories. I have known rabbis in Jerusalem who quoted from Jasher to explain certain details of Jewish history that are not extensively detailed in the Torah. For example, there is a story in sacred Jewish history that tells about the birth of Abraham and his link to a certain cosmic event.

Nimrod was the builder of several early cities, chiefly Babel. Located in the area of modern Iraq, the central building was the tower of Babel (Genesis 11). Historically, Nimrod was living around the time of a noted man named Terah, the father of Abraham. The book of Jasher says:

> "And when all the wise men and conjurors went out from the house of Terah, they lifted up their eyes toward heaven that night to look at the stars, and they saw, and behold one very large star came from the east and ran into the heavens and swallowed up four stars from the four sides of heaven…"
>
> "And they said to each other, "This only betokens the child that has been born to Terah this night, will grow up to be fruitful, and multiply, and possess all the earth, he and his children forever, and his seed shall slay great kings, and inherit their lands."
>
> –Jasher VII, 1-5.

Years later, God instructed Abraham to look to the stars of heaven and predicted that the number of Abraham's future children would become so great that they would be innumerable, just as the stars of heaven cannot be numbered (Genesis 15:5).

In the Days of Joseph

Joseph, the son of Jacob, was sold by his brothers to the Ishmaelites, who sold him to an Egyptian as a slave. By interpreting a warning dream, he was exalted by Pharaoh as second-in-command over the land of Egypt. Joseph eventually married the daughter of an Egyptian priest named Asenath (Genesis 41:45). Scripture says that Joseph had a silver cup used for divining, or revealing the future (Genesis 44:2). This cup would have been given to Joseph by Pharaoh in exchange for Joseph interpreting the dream. However, there is no record that it was ever used or needed, since Joseph was directed by the Spirit of God.

In the days of Sesostris II (1906-1887 BC), the priest of Heilopolis had a vision that he recorded. The words appear to be a prediction:

"The ideal ruler for whose advent he longs—he brings cooling to the flames. It is said he is the shepherd of all men. There is no evil in his heart...where is he today...behold his might is not seen."

The Hebrews were shepherds, and Egyptians hated shepherds (Genesis 46:34). When Joseph requested that his brothers meet Pharaoh, he instructed them to say, "We raise cattle." Perhaps Joseph was fearful that Pharaoh would not allow his family to live in Egypt had he known their occupation. The brothers instead chose to reveal that they were shepherds.

There was also an ancient prediction mentioned by the Jewish historian Josephus concerning a lamb that would defeat Egypt:

"Pharaoh slept, and saw in his sleep a balance, and behold the whole land of Egypt stood in one scale, and a lamb in the other;

and the scale in which the lamb was, outweighed that in which was the land of Egypt. Immediately he sent and called all the chief magicians, and told them his dream. And Jannes and Jambres (see 2 Timothy 3:8), who were chief of the magicians, opened their mouths and said to Pharaoh, 'A child is shortly to be born in the congregation of the Israelites whose hand shall destroy the whole land of Egypt.' Therefore Pharaoh spake to the midwives, etc.

"One of those sacred Scribes (said to be Jannes or Jambres in the Targum of Jonathan) who are very sagacious in foretelling future events, truly told the king that about this time there would be a child born to the Israelites, who as he were reared, would bring Egyptian domain low, and would raise the Israelites: that he would excel all men in virtue, and obtain a glory that would be remembered though the ages…which thing was so feared by the king, that according to this man's opinion, he commanded that they should cast every male child which was born to the Israelites, into the river and destroy it…that if any parents should disobey him and venture to save their male children alive, they and their families should be destroyed."

– *Josephus Antiquities*; Book II, Chapter IX

It would truly be a lamb that would defeat the entire empire of Egypt. The Passover lambs were offered prior to the Exodus (Exodus 12), and the blood was placed in the left, right, and top outer parts of the door to prevent the destroyer from taking the life of the firstborn sons. The lamb was then roasted and eaten, bringing healing to the entire Hebrew nation all in one night (Psalm 105:37).

Cosmic Signs at Moses' Birth

Three years before the birth of Moses, a conjunction of Jupiter and Saturn occurred in the constellation Pisces (the fish), which has always been considered a sign of the nation of the Hebrews (Israel). This was interpreted as a sign that a great person would be born among the Jews. Some rabbis suggest that this was the motive for Pharaoh instructing the midwives to kill male children by throwing them into the Nile River (Exodus 1:22). The alligator was one of the gods of Egypt, and slaying the Hebrew infants could serve as an offering to an Egyptian god. But God had the final word when, about eighty years later, the Egyptian army was drowned in the Red Sea (Exodus 12 and 13).

Signs Among the Roman Emperors

Julius Caesar was the first emperor of imperial Rome. He passed laws that caused people to move from one location to another, and one such group was colonists from Capua. Ancient graves and vessels of these people were found in their original homeland, along with a monument of the founder of Capua. That monument included a bronze tablet written in Greek with the prediction:

"When once the houses of Capys are brought to light, then a branch of the Julian house will be slain by the hand of one of his kindred; his death however, will soon be avenged by terrible occurrences in Italy."

Julius Caesar's wife had a troubling dream that their home fell apart, and she warned her husband not to go to the coliseum. He ignored the warning and was stabbed twenty-three times, dying in 44 BC at age fifty-five. Thus the strange prediction made years before came to pass.

Caesar Augustus was the emperor at the time of Christ's birth. His father, Octavius, consulted a local oracle about his son. When wine libation was poured upon the altar, the fire leaped to the roof of the temple. The priest told Octavius that his son would achieve greatness, adding that this had happened only one other time, when Alexander the Great was sacrificing.

At the time of Christ's birth, Rome was celebrating its 750th anniversary. Caesar Augustus was conducting celebrations and everyone was taxed to help pay the bill for the celebrations (Luke 2:1). Augustus soon considered himself the "prince of peace," and he built a huge temple after being told that he would rise to imperial power.

Roman emperors often sought out advice from individuals through what was known as oracles. An oracle was either a person who gave counsel or predictions, or the site where the utterance was given. One such place was Palatine hill, located at the centermost hill of the seven hills of ancient Rome. Augustus went to Delphic oracles to ask how long his temple of peace that he built would last. The oracle revealed, "Until a virgin gives birth to a child and yet remains a virgin."

Thinking that it was impossible for a virgin to birth a child, Augustus was certain his temple would endure forever. He dedicated his own temple with the inscription, Templum Pacis Aeternae, thus indicating that this would be a temple of peace that would endure eternally. However, true to the oracle's prediction, at the time of Christ's birth the temple collapsed without cause upon its foundation.

The Roman Senate had declared that Augustus was god of the nation, so Augustus wanted to know if a greater prince than he would ever be born. During his consultation with an oracle, a meteorite suddenly lit the dark sky and the woman put down her books and said to Augustus, "It is a sign of the future which is revealed to you. One world is ending and another is beginning."

From the ancients' perspective, she was referring to a 2,150 year cycle of Aires the Ram and the inception of a cosmic "sign" of Pisces the fish in the procession of the equinoxes. This happened at the same moment this oracle was given:

"A child has just been born, who is the king of the future millennia, the true God of the world. He is of humble birth and of obscure race. His divinity is unrealized; when he at last makes himself known, he will be persecuted. He will work miracles; he will be accused of trafficking with evil spirits. But I see him as victor in the end over death, rising from the place where His murderers entombed him. He will reunite all nations."

Caesar Augustus reported this story to the Senate, and they placed the record in the Roman archives. The oracle was read hundreds of years later at the time when Constantine became the emperor.

Cosmic Activity at Christ's Birth

While astrology in the form that we know it today is forbidden in Scriptures; and while God prohibits the worship of the sun, moon and stars; and while He forbids the notion that the stars control your life, still the heavenly hosts were created by God and were looked upon for "signs and seasons." The sun cycle determines the year, the moon cycles determine the month, and the stars are positioned as visual pictures. According to Josephus, the sons of Seth were given insight into the heavens and the heavenly cycles, and that information was further revealed to Enoch. Those in ancient days were often moved by what they saw occurring in the heavens, whether those things were eclipses, meteorites, comets, or the positioning of certain planets.

Even the best of scholars differ as to the exact time of Christ's birth, but there is historical evidence that 2 BC was very significant from a prophetic perspective. There are some important points to bring out in the gospel narrative of Christ's birth in Bethlehem:

1. Caesar Augustus was the Emperor (Luke 2:1)
3. A new tax was being introduced (Luke 2:1)
4. A strange cosmic alignment was occurring (Matthew 2:2)

When the Jews were in Babylon, prophets such as Daniel studied scrolls from other Hebrew prophets, such as Jeremiah (Daniel 9:2). The first five books of Moses, called the Torah, were also carried by the Jews into the nations where they were in captivity. This explains how the Magi, a group of Persian star gazers, would have understood that a king was being born among the Jews somewhere in Palestine (Israel). The prediction of this comic sign is recorded in Scripture:

> *"I see Him, but not now; I behold Him, but not near; a Star shall come out of Jacob; a Scepter shall rise out of Israel, and batter the brow of Moab, and destroy all the sons of tumult."*
>
> —Numbers 24:17

This unique prophecy indicates that a star arises out of Jacob, also identified as Israel (the name that Jacob received after wrestling with the angel in Genesis 32:28). The Hebrew word for scepter is shebet, and it alludes to a branch of a tree or a rod that was used by a ruler. When the Magi came to Jerusalem they informed Herod, "We have seen his star in the east" (Matthew 2:2). What was His star? What did they see?

Among the ancients, the study of the heavens, planets, and stars were important in every nation. They would observe eclipses, comets, and the alignment of certain planets within the constellations and read them as important cosmic signs indicating events and special births on earth.

Among the planets and constellations were several in the Roman period that are prophetically significant. Jupiter was considered the planet of King David, while Venus was identified as the bright and morning star. Venus is often the brightest and most common object to be seen in the heavens, just before sunrise. Then there are numerous constellations that also carry a prophetic meaning. For example, the emblem of the tribe of Judah is a lion (Genesis 49:9-10). In the heavens there are twelve major constellations in the imaginary circle called the ecliptic; one is called Leo the Lion, which is the constellation representing Judah. Any cosmic sign connecting Jupiter with Leo could have been interpreted as a sign of the coming Messiah.

A cosmic event occurred between 3-2 BC that may answer the question, "What was the star of the Jewish King?" Within the constellation of the Lion (Leo) there is a major star called Regulus—a king star, according to Hellenistic tradition. Between 3-2 BC there were seven conjunctions that occurred; three were between Jupiter and Regulus, and one was a very close conjunction between the planet and Venus around June 17, 2 BC.

The wise men that brought gold, frankincense, and myrrh to Jesus, may have done so based upon a prediction by the Hebrew prophet Isaiah:

> *"And the Gentiles shall come to thy light, and kings to the brightness of thy rising. The multitude of camels shall cover thee, the dromedaries of Median and Ephah; all they from Sheba shall come: they shall bring gold and incense; and they shall shew forth the praises of the LORD."* —Isaiah 60:3 and 6 (KJV)

The Year 2 BC

For many years there have been varied opinions as to the actual birth date of Christ. While the traditional date is celebrated as December 25, the Orthodox churches in the east celebrate it several weeks later on January 6th (Armenian) or 7th (Eastern Orthodox) on the Julian calendar. Many scholars and Messianic believers place the date of Christ's birth during the seasons of the fall feast, such as Trumpets or Tabernacles.

It is clear in the New Testament that there was an expectation that the arrival of Israel's Messiah was near. In Daniel chapter 9, the prophet revealed a prophetic timeframe of seventy weeks of years, or four-hundred-ninety years that would "finish the transgression, make an end to sin, bring in everlasting righteousness, and anoint the most holy" (Daniel 9:24). Daniel even mentions the Messiah the prince in Daniel 9:25-26. Over four hundred years had passed since Daniel's prophecy, and there was increased anticipation of the Messiah's arrival.

This anticipation is also evident in a Biblical narrative when an old rabbi named Simeon entered the Temple at the time when the special offering was being presented to the Temple priest for the birth of a son.

> *"And behold, there was a man in Jerusalem whose name was Simeon, and this man was just and devout, waiting for the Consolation*

of Israel, and the Holy Spirit was upon him. And it had been revealed to him by the Holy Spirit that he would not see death before he had seen the Lord's Christ." —Luke 2:25-27

Simon saw the infant Christ, gave a dramatic prophecy over the child, and then requested, "Now Lord, let your servant depart (this life) in peace, for my eyes have seen your salvation that you have prepared for the face of all people..." (Luke 2:29-31). As Simeon was speaking, an eighty-four year old prophetess named Anna approached the child. She, too, recognized Him as the Savior and Messiah. Scripture records, "And coming in that instant she gave thanks to the Lord, and spoke of Him to all those who looked for redemption in Jerusalem" (Luke 2:38).

Not only were the prophetically sensitive saints living in anticipation of the time of Christ's birth, there also were numerous events taking place in the secular realm that indicated the "fullness of time" (Galatians 4:4). The Roman historian Tactius wrote:

> "A persuasion existed in the minds of many that some ancient writings of the priests contained a prediction that about that time an eastern power would prevail, and that persons proceeding from Judea would obtain dominion."

Events at 2 BC

Astronomers and historians note that there were various cosmic signs from 7 BC to 2 BC that could have been interpreted by ancient star observers as signs of the birth of royalty. In 7 BC there was a triple conjunction of Jupiter and Saturn in the constellation Pisces, which is considered to be the heavenly body representing the nation of Israel. Then in 6 BC, there was a near-conjunction of Mars, Jupiter, and Saturn in Pisces. To the Jews, the fact that these planets met in the symbol of the two fish was a significant event, since a triple conjunction as the one in 7 BC occurs only once every nine hundred years. The conjunction of Mars, Jupiter, and Saturn within eight degrees of one another occurs about once every eight hundred years. These events would have gained the attention of those observing the times.

In 2 BC, however, many events occurred. As stated previously, the Roman Empire was celebrating its 750th year anniversary. The year also marked the twenty-fifth-year reign of Caesar Augustus. This was the year that Augustus was named "father of the nation" and even "prince of peace." In order to pay for the celebrations, each family had to return to the place of their family origin to register their names in a census and pay the required tax (Luke 2:3).

For this reason, Mary and Joseph, he being from the linage of King David, traveled from Nazareth to Bethlehem (Luke 2:4-5). The reason there was no room in the inn when they arrived (Luke 2:7) is because so many people whose families originated from the tribe of Judah in Bethlehem were registering in the city. Part of the census was to swear an oath that a person would not form a revolt or attempt to overthrow Rome. Perhaps this is why Herod was so upset that a Jewish King would be born in the same city as Israel's most famous King, David.

The cosmic events, significant dates of the Roman Empire, and anticipation among rabbis of the imminent appearance of the Messiah, seem to point a 2 to 1 BC birth of Christ.

As you can see, as far back as the Egyptian empire, people consulted men that were believed to have a gift of foretelling future events, often by discerning the patterns of the planets and their positioning in the heavens. Among the ancient cultures were the famed Mayan Indians, whose predictions are now being revived and reviewed by secular writers and modern prognosticators.

CHAPTER 3

Prophecies Among the Ancient Indians

Long before fair-skinned Europeans arrived on the shores of America, there were Indian tribes living in specific regions of North and South America. It is interesting to note that even the Indians had individuals who made future predictions. In Christian theology, all prophecy points to a timeline ending in a final battle in Israel that is called Armageddon, and the sudden return of the Messiah to save Israel and the Jewish remnant (Revelation 12:17; 16:16; 19:15). The Indians, however, predicted that events would move in great cycles. The cycle method is actually the more proper method of viewing prophecy.

In the Bible we read that Christ is the beginning and the end (Revelation 21:6 and 22:13). The beginning was at the creation of Adam in the Garden of Eden, and the ending will be when the New Jerusalem descends and we enter eternity, where time as we know it will cease (Revelation 10:6). Christians know the past, live in the present, and anticipate the future by discerning the signs of the times (Matthew 16:3). We see time as being a straight line that has a beginning, a mid-point, and a conclusion. Special events are pre-planned by God to occur on this time line. Some events have been revealed through scripture, while others will remain a mystery until they are witnessed as we enter a period of time called a "season." During these seasons, both minor and major events occur that will impact those living at that time. This is called linear time, and it is a Greek way of viewing the progression of time.

The second method of observing time is called comparative time. This is when two parallel events occur at the same time. For example, the Turks took Jerusalem in 1517, which was the same year that Martin Luther began his reformation movement in Germany. Four hundred years later, in 1917, World War I concluded and the Turks lost control of Jerusalem and Palestine to the British. The same year, the Balfour Declaration was signed, giving the Jews access back to Palestine. There were also seven eclipses that occurred the same year. These are events that occur at the same time, giving us the ability to compare these events in light of prophetic scenarios and fulfillment.

Ancient cultures, however, understood that time was a circle. It had a beginning, and each cycle had an ending that initiated a new cycle. This concept is understood in Hebraic teaching, such as when Solomon wrote in Ecclesiastes 1:9-10, "The thing that has been is that which shall be, and that which has been done is that which shall be done (in the future). This is why it is often said that history repeats itself. This repeat is simply another cycle manifesting with the same patterns of a previous cycle. One of the most interesting cycles of our time is seen with the Abraham Lincoln and John Kennedy presidencies and their assassinations:

- Lincoln was elected in 1860 and Kennedy in 1960.
- Both Vice Presidents were named Johnson.
- Andrew Johnson was born in 1808 and Lyndon Johnson in 1908.

- John Wilkes booth was born in 1839 and Lee Harvey Oswald in 1939.
- Lincoln and Kennedy each have seven letters in their last name.
- John Wilkes Booth and Lee Harvey Oswald have 15 letters in their names.
- Andrew Johnson and Lyndon Johnson have 13 letters in their names.
- Both Vice Presidents were southern Democratic Senators before being elected.
- Both presidents had their election contested.
- Both presidents were involved in Civil Rights.
- Both presidents were congressmen (1846 and 1946) before becoming presidents.
- Both foresaw their deaths before they occurred.
- Both were shot on Friday.
- Both were shot in the head.
- Both were shot in the presence of their wives.
- Both experienced the death of a child while in the White House.
- Lincoln's secretary was named Kennedy and Kennedy's was named Lincoln.
- Both secretaries warned the presidents not to go to the place where they were later killed.

- A southern radical shot each president.
- Lincoln was shot in a theater; the killer hid in a warehouse: Kennedy was shot from a book warehouse and the killer hid in a theater.
- Lincoln was shot in Ford's Theater and Kennedy was shot in a Ford Lincoln Limousine.
- Both assassins were killed before they stood trial.

This is one of the premier examples of history moving in a circle, then repeating the event at another time and in another place. In the realm of Biblical prophecy, I have discovered through many hours of study that major events which occur in contemporary time and impact the world in general or Israel specifically, have already occurred in the form of historical, political, and spiritual reflections, or cycles. Viewing time through cycles of history is at the center of the Mayan Indian teaching.

The Mayan Indians

The Mayan Indians were extremely advanced in math, writing, and astronomy. When we think of pyramids, we think of the great pyramid structures in Egypt, one of the world's oldest civilizations. However, the same type of pyramid structure is also found among the ruins of the ancient Mayan Indians. It is believed that the idea of the circle was invented by those living in ancient Mesopotamia (now southern Iraq) who were known as Sumerians, Akkadians, and Babylonians. Over 4400 hundred years ago they invented primitive writing and the 360-degree circle. Twenty-four-hundred years ago, the calendars consisted of twelve months of thirty days each, or 360 days making a complete solar cycle (one year). Around 1500 BC, the Egyptians divided the day into twenty-four hours. Several hundred years before Christ, the Babylonians divided time into sixty minutes per hour, and sixty seconds per minute.

It is clear from secular history that the Babylonians, Egyptians, and Hebrews were aware of rain and harvest cycles, and that they established calendars that were effective for both secular and religious purposes. These three cultures all lived in the same area of the world and had access to information passed down from generation to generation, so they gleaned from one another to understand cosmic activity, calendars, and time. However, how did the Mayan Indians, who lived in the Yucatan Peninsula thousands of years ago, tap into one of the most accurate calendars of any people group in the world?

The Mayan Pyramid

In Yucatan, Mexico is the famous Mayan pyramid called the Pyramid of Kukulkan at Chichen Itza, built in 1050 AD. The face of the pyramid has four stairways, each with ninety-one steps. With the shared steps of the platform on top, the number of steps totals 365, the same number of days on a solar calendar.

The Mayan's used a week of thirteen days that were numbered from one to thirteen. They used a named week of twenty days, and each day was given a name. They also used a civil calendar of eighteen months of twenty days each, adding five days at the end of the count to make 365 days.

The Mayan calendar uses three forms of counts in their dating system: the long count, the tzolkin (divine count), and the habb (civil calendar).

To simplify some very long and complicated research, when using their long count:

- 1 uinal is 20 kin, or 20 days
- 1 tun is 18 unial of 360 days, which is about 1 year
- 1 katun is 20 tuns or 7,200 days, which is about 20 years
- 1 baktun is 20 katun or 144,000 days, or about 394 years

There are Mayan timeframes that are even longer that those mentioned above. They extend from 158,000 to 63 million years, which is labeled one alautm. There is disagreement as to when the long count actually started. The interest in the Mayan calendar and the "end of the age" or the "end of time" is linked to the conclusion of a long count cycle on the Mayan calendar.

The long count began August 11, 3114 BC and the cycle will be completed on December 2012 AD. This day marks a major 5,126 year cycle and is the conclusion of a long count cycle.

It is difficult to get non-Christians to read books on Biblical prophecy, as they view Christian prophetic teaching as some weird, extreme viewpoint that is out of the mainstream. These same people, however, will read books that deal with New Age prophecies by secular writers that have no divine inspiration. The same is true with the predictions of the Mayans.

Some of their predictions are as follows. Every twenty years is a katun; the most recent runs from 1992 to 2010. It is said to be a "time of no time," when the solar winds intensify. Seven years later is a time when the world is to enter the "sacred hall of mirrors," a time of darkness when men will see how they have lived and what they have done. They expected that there will be many solar eclipses and planetary alignments. The alleged 7th world begins in 2012, when the plane of our Solar System will line up with the plane of our galaxy.

Why All the Concern?

When simply looking at this cycle, it appears that one cycle ends and another cycle begins. But there are people who see another possibility, and this is the cause for concern. On the winter solstice in 2012, scientists say that the sun will be aligned with the center of the Milky Way for the first time in about 26,000 years. This means that whatever energy typically streams to earth from the center of the Milky Way may be disrupted on 12/21/12 at 11:11. Some believe the sunspot cycles could wreck havoc on the Earth's magnetic field and our own atmosphere, creating earthquakes and severe power outages around the world.

When hearing about, then later researching the varied opinions of 2012, I was reminded of a prediction made in 1981 that struck fear in the hearts of many. As a young minister who was interested in Biblical prophecy, I read every prophetic book and periodical I could find. In a 32-page booklet entitled *The Parade of the Planets*, the authors noted that in 1981 the planets were aligning in one straight line, or a string. Several experts suggested that this unique alignment would have a negative impact on earth and create stress on the planet, disrupting electro-magnetic fields, creating stress fractures that would cause massive earthquakes, and thereby introducing an apocalyptic scenario throughout the world. I was young and devoured the book, then began telling close friends to prepare for what might happen. When 1982 came, the universe was completely intact, the earth was spinning as normal, and life continued.

That is when I learned that there is a difference between someone's prophetic opinion, speculation, and scientific facts. Everyone who writes about the year 2012 will say, "We do not know what, if anything, will happen." I suggest that we can turn to the Scriptures and say that one day there will be famines, pestilence, and earthquakes in different places (Luke 21:11). These events will occur because we are entering the seasons of the birth pains that precede the arrival of the Messiah (Matthew 24:8), because creation itself is in travail (Romans 8:22), and because man is destroying the earth through chemicals, weapons of mass destruction, and pollution (Revelations 11:18).

Luke recorded the words of Christ as He warned of the famines, earthquakes, and pestilences. He also mentioned that Christ said there would be fearful signs and great signs from heaven (Luke 21:11). A fearful sign would be a warning that an asteroid, meteorite, or a comet was heading into earth's atmosphere and was on a collision course with the planet. Some of the great signs would, in my opinion, be the many unusual cosmic signs that are considered by ancient Jewish Rabbis to be spiritual indicators. In the next chapter we will look at some of these cosmic signs.

CHAPTER 4

Cosmic Signs Linked to Israel and the Year 2015

The calendar of ancient Israel is linked to the cycles of the moon and not just to the sun. Israel uses a lunar-solar calendar. The moon has a cycle that goes from full to dark and back to full in 29 ½ days. In approximately fifteen days, the moon has moved from dark to full, and within another fifteen days from full back to dark. A rabbinical teaching reveals that there were fifteen generations from Abraham, when the darkness was upon the earth, to Solomon, when the moon was full and the nations of the earth saw God's glory in Israel. After Solomon's death, however, within fifteen generations Israel began a slow decline. They moved from Solomon, the light of Israel, to Babylonian captivity, when Israel fell into spiritual bondage and darkness!

Since Israel's calendar was based upon moon cycles, then any cosmic activity involving the moon was considered a message to Israel. Joel prophesied that the sun would be darkened and the moon turn to blood before the great and terrible day of the Lord (Joel 2:10-11). This prophecy was repeated on the Day of Pentecost by the Apostle Peter (Acts 2:20).

When I was a child I heard a minister preach about the time of the end when the sun would be dark and the moon would turn to blood.

One elderly woman in our church believed that the moon turning into blood indicated a war that would occur on the moon when the Russians and the American's would land space crafts at the same time, and a fight would ensue. Since there is no gravity and the astronauts would be wearing space suits, I am uncertain how they would kill one another. Can you image a Russian floating around in space while swinging a sword and attempting to pierce the suit of the American? Skeptics often hear such passages and laugh, because the literal sun could never be darkened, as the darkness would eventually destroy all plant life on earth. Neither are we expecting the sun to burn out anytime soon. I always felt there was another interpretation to this passage, but could never find the answer until I went to Israel in November 1996, during the 3000th year anniversary of Jerusalem.

During this special anniversary, two lunar eclipses were seen over Jerusalem. The first fell on Passover, April 3, 1996, and was a full lunar eclipse, causing the moon to appear to be a red-orange color. The Jerusalem Post published a picture of the moon with the caption, "blood moon." A second, ninety percent lunar eclipse occurred over the city on September 26-27, 1996 on the eve of the Feast of Tabernacles. Several months later on March 3, 1997, a third lunar eclipse occurred on the Feast of Purim.

Three lunar eclipses occurred within a one year period of time, all on or near significant Jewish feasts day. I discovered that a total solar eclipse is called a sackcloth sun, while a lunar eclipse is considered by ancient rabbis to be a blood moon, because the moon appears like blood to the human eye. I learned that these eclipses represent an important message from God when they occur on Jewish feast days.

The Jewish Talmud has a lot to say on the subject of lunar eclipses. Sukkah 29a reads, "When the moon is in eclipse, it is a bad omen for Israel…if the face is as red as blood, (it is a sign) the sword is coming to the world…"

The rabbis taught, "When the sun is in eclipse it is a bad omen for the world." Another observation is made by Rabbi Meir who said, "When the luminaries are in eclipse, it is a bad omen for Israel." According to the rabbinical interpretation of eclipses, a solar eclipse is a sign of trouble for the world and a lunar eclipse is a bad sign for Israel. The most eclipses that can occur in one year are seven. Twice in the twentieth century there were seven total eclipses, in 1917 and 1973. Both years were filled with prophetic implications.

In the future there will be a series of lunar eclipses, or blood moons, which will fall on major Jewish feast cycles. In the five books of Moses (the Torah), God established various cycles that are repeated on a weekly, monthly, or yearly basis. For example, each seventh day was a continual cycle of Sabbath rest (Exodus 20:10). Each seventh year was a Jubilee Sabbath in which the land was to rest from tilling and planting the seed (Leviticus 25:4). Every forty-nine years, or seven Sabbaths of seven years each, was a major time known as the Jubilee. This fell on the seventh month, the tenth day of the month, and was announced by blowing the silver trumpets (Leviticus 25).

Almost all major prophetic events linked to Christ have been or likely will be fulfilled on the major feast days of Israel. For example, there are seven major feasts established in the Torah. Christ has fulfilled three spring feasts, the Holy Spirit and birth of the church has fulfilled one, and future prophetic events will, I believe, occur on or during the three final feasts, all which are celebrated in the fall months of September or October, depending upon how the Jewish calendar months fall.

The Feast of Israel Fulfillment (English Name)	The Fulfillment or Future
• Passover	Christ, the Lamb of God, was crucified
• Unleavened Bread	Christ, the sinless sacrifice, was in the tomb
• First Fruits	Christ was raised from the dead as the first fruits
• Pentecost	The Holy Spirit was sent and the Church was birthed
• Trumpets	Possibly the time of the rapture and resurrection
• Atonement	Possibly the time of the tribulation and judgments
• Tabernacles	Possibly the time when Christ returns to Jerusalem

Since Israel is on the lunar calendar, then any sign linked to the moon that occurs on a Jewish feast date is considered an important omen for Israel. Here is a brief history of eclipses:

- September 27, 14 AD — the death of Caesar Augustus

- April 3, 33 AD — possible time of the crucifixion

- March 4, 71 AD — the plowing of Jerusalem with salt by the Romans

- May 22, 1453 — the fall of Constantinople to the Muslims
- March 1, 1504 — called the Columbus eclipse
- July 31, 1776 — after America's independence from Britain
- January 15, 1805 — the Lewis and Clark expedition
- July 4, 1917 — the timeframe of World War I and the Balfour Declaration

Among the ancients, solar eclipses often brought superstition and fear. The ancient Chinese believed that solar eclipses were heavenly signs that foretold the birth of future emperors and leaders. One of the famous eclipses occurred on January 27, 632 and was visible in Medina, Arabia. This was significant since Mohammad, the founder of Islam, had been expelled from Mecca and was living with his followers in Medina. It was the year 632, the same year of the eclipse, that the founder of Islam died.

Blood Moons over Israel

There are significant dates and months on the Jewish calendar. The first month when three of the yearly spring feasts occur is called Nissan. Three of the yearly fall feasts occur on Tishrei, the seventh month. One of the most noted times on the Jewish calendar is the month of Av. The ninth day of Av is considered one of the worst days for the Jewish people. According to Jewish history, the following events occurred on the 9th of Av:

- Twelve spies returned with the bad report;
- The Exodus generation was condemned to die;

- Nebuchadnezzar set fire to the first Temple;
- Romans destroyed the second Temple;
- Romans plowed up the Temple Mount to convert Jerusalem to a Roman colony;
- The last Jewish revolt (Bar Kokba) was squelched;
- King Edward expelled the Jews in 1290 AD;
- Turkey banned the immigration of Russian Jews;
- A decree to expel Jews from parts of Hungary in 1941.

No wonder the Jews fast on the 9th of Av! When Christopher Columbus was set to sail in 1492, the ships were prepared to leave the dock on the 9th of Av. There were Jewish men on the ship, and Columbus postponed the trip until the following day. Perhaps he simply chose not to travel on a Jewish fast day. Or perhaps he was informed it would be a bad omen to begin his journey on such a potentially dangerous day. It is interesting that Columbus and his men spotted land on the last day of the Feasts of Tabernacles.

According to the NASA web site that projects the dates of partial and total eclipses, a series of partial and total eclipses occurred or will occur in 2008, 2009, and 2010. All are on the first two days of the month of Av:

- Av 1 – August 2008
- Av 2 – August 2009
- Av 1 – August 2010

Pastor Mark Blitz of El Shaddai Ministries in Bonney Lake, Washington has done the following research on the link between the eclipses and the feasts. Since Israel is on a lunar calendar and the moon is a symbol of the nation (Genesis 37:9-10), then a blood moon is interpreted as an omen linked to Israel. In 1996 the lunar eclipse occurred on both Passover and Tabernacles, and this has happened a total of seven times on both of these feasts, from 1 AD to 1996. Double blood moons were seen at or near Passover in 1493, after the Jews had been expelled from Spain and Columbus was discovering the new land. The dates are:

- Passover — April 2, 1493
- Tabernacles — September 25, 1493
- Passover — March 22, 1494
- Tabernacles — September 15, 1494

In 1949 and 1950, the same lunar eclipses were repeated during the season when Israel was being rebirthed as a nation, and when Arab nations initiated a war of independence as they attempted to defeat the young Jewish state. The dates were:

- Passover — April 13, 1949
- Tabernacles — October 7, 1949
- Passover — April 2, 1950
- Tabernacles — September 26, 1950

More lunar eclipses occurred in the years 1966-67, which was a major prophetic year:

- First day of Passover   – April 24, 1967
- First day of Tabernacles – October 18, 1967
- First day of Passover   – April 13, 1968
- First day of Tabernacles – October 6, 1968

During the Six Day War between Israel and surrounding Arab nations, the lunar eclipses appeared again. On June 7, 1967, the third day of the war, East Jerusalem was taken and later annexed by Israel.

The seventh series of lunar eclipses happened in 1996, and the 8th series will occur between 2014 and 2015. Pastor Mark Blitz says, "The Jewish religious year will begin with a total solar eclipse, and two weeks later a total **lunar** eclipse on Passover. The civil year (Rosh Hashanah) begins with a solar eclipse, followed two weeks later by another **blood moon** on the feast of Tabernacles."

- First Day of Passover   – April 15, 2014
- First Day of Tabernacles – October 8, 2014
- First Day of Passover   – April 4, 2015
- First Day of Tabernacles – September 28, 2015

Modern history in particular seems to bear out the belief that the blood moon is a sign linked to Israel, and is often accompanied by a breakthrough for the nation or a major conflict with her enemies. Most prophetic scholars are aware that one of the future wars of prophecy is a conflict with an Islamic coalition on the mountains of Israel. That conflict, spoken of in Ezekiel 38 and 39, is identified as the war of Gog and Magog. It will be interesting to see whether the lunar eclipses and the blood moon occur close to the time of this prophetic war.

CHAPTER 5

Living During the Birth Pains of the Messiah

"For nation shall rise against nation, and kingdom against kingdom: and there shall be famines, and pestilences, and earthquakes in divers places. All these are the beginning of sorrows."

—Matthew 24:7-8 (KJV)

In these verses, Christ was informing His disciples of the signs that would precede the destruction of the Jewish Temple in Jerusalem, and signs that would occur prior to His return to earth to set up the kingdom in Jerusalem. This sermon, called the Olivet Discourse, takes the disciples and reader through a time tunnel that begins with the destruction of Jerusalem, then continues through the preaching of the gospel around the world, the abomination of the antichrist, the great tribulation, and cosmic signs. The sermon ends with the return of Christ to rule and reign on earth!

As Christ spoke of the initial signs of famine, pestilence, and earthquakes in different places, He revealed an important message when He said, "All these things must come to pass, but the end is not yet" (Matthew 24:6). Christ immediately changed the signs from natural disasters, to signs of nations and entire kingdoms being overthrown and shaken by wars and rumors of wars. Following this revelation Christ said, "All of these are the beginning of sorrows."

There are several different meanings for the word "sorrow" throughout the New Testament. These include grief (Luke 22:45), pain and distress (Romans 9:2), mourning (Revelation 18:7), inner pain (Acts 20:38), and birth pains. The English Bible mentions sorrows, which was a word used in earlier centuries to mean birth pains. The Greek word for sorrows is *odin*, which means "travail and birth pains."

In the Old Testament, the "Day of the Lord," which refers to the time of the end and the future tribulation, is identified with the imagery of a woman in travail, giving birth to a man child (Isaiah 13:8; 26:17-18; Jeremiah 22:23; 48:41). The common root word for the Hebrew word travail has a connotation of entering into labor with fear and trembling. In Judaism, the travail preceding the Day of the Lord is considered the "birth pains of the Messiah."

Christ Himself made it clear that the beginning of these labor pains would be marked by the sign of wars and rumors of wars. In the New Testament Greek, Matthew 24:7 reads that "ethnos eppa ethnos" and "basileia eppa basileia." The word ethnos alludes to non-Jewish, or Gentile nations, rising up against other Gentile nations. In modern English we would say that "ethnic group will battle ethnic group." There are certainly many internal struggles and small wars occurring among ethnic groups. The Greek word for kingdom is often used to refer to a kingdom controlled by royalty. However, throughout much of Europe, the Catholic churches are called "Basilica," which is a Latin word. Again, using our contemporary understanding of how this word is used, we could say that religion will be fighting religion. This is evident with

1. Mayan Pyramid in Mexico – In the Yucatan area of Mexico sits a famous Mayan pyramid called the Pyramid of Kukulkan at Chichen Itza, built in 1050 AD. The pyramid has four stairways, each with 91 steps and a platform on top totaling 365, the same number of days on a solar calendar.

2. Lunar Eclipse – Jewish rabbis consider a total lunar eclipse to be a Biblical "blood moon" (Joel 2:31). A lunar eclipse is a bad omen for Israel. In 2014 and 2015, four lunar eclipses will occur on Jewish feast days. A rare occurrence indeed!

3. 1999 Leonid Meteorite (it looks like a sword) – Josephus described a "star shaped like a sword" that stood over Jerusalem before its destruction. This event may have been a meteor shower, as witnessed in Italy. In 1998, these meteorites formed a sword shape in the constellation Leo the Lion.

4. Otzi the Iceman – The famous "iceman," found under ice in Italy and killed in 3300 BC, was marked several places with tattoos in the form of a plus sign or a cross, which was one of the earliest symbols of protection.

5. Asteroid – The apocalypse predicts a "star will fall from heaven" and destroy a third of the earth. The word "star" alludes to an asteroid that will suddenly hit and bring major destruction during the Great Tribulation.

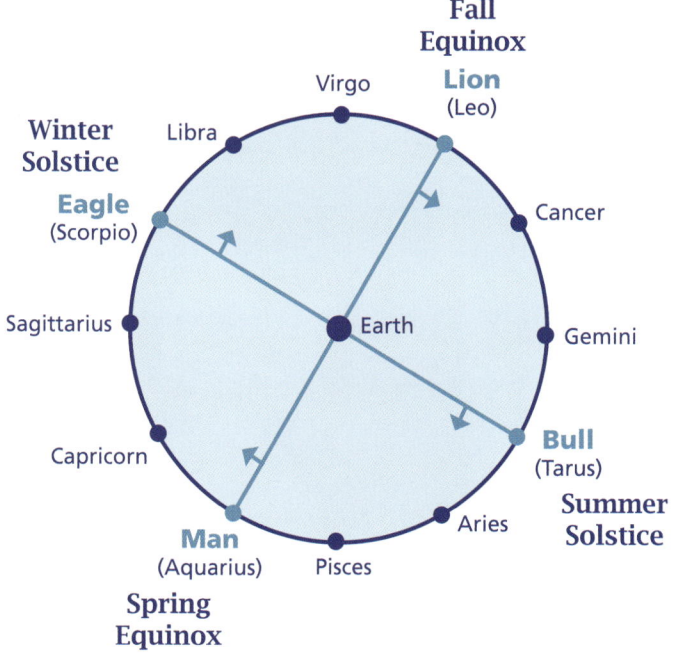

6. The Grand Cross – The "Grand Cross" is a term to describe the position of eight planets that aligned in a cross formation in the constellations of the lion (Leo), the bull (Taurus), the man (Aquarius), and the eagle (Scorpio). These emblems match the four living creatures around the throne of God in heaven (Rev. 4:7).

7. The "Atom Smasher" – Some scientists are concerned about the Hadron Collider, a huge machine that will smash atoms to create a mini "big bang." Some suggest the machine could actually create a black hole on earth!

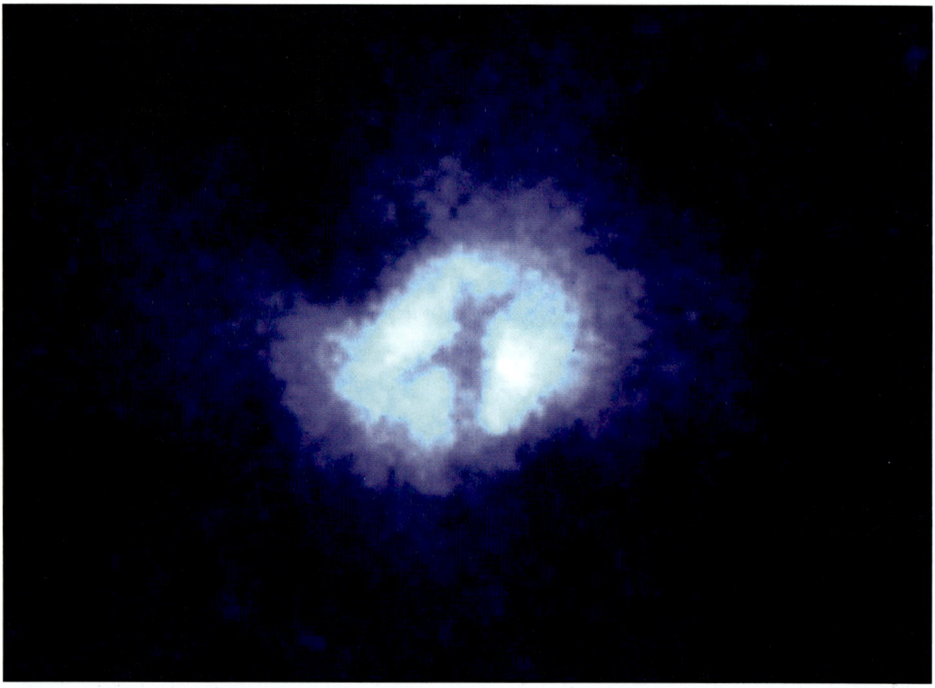

8. The Cross in the Whirlpool Galaxy – The black hole in the center of the Whirlpool Galaxy consists of a mixture of gasses that uniquely form the image of a cross.

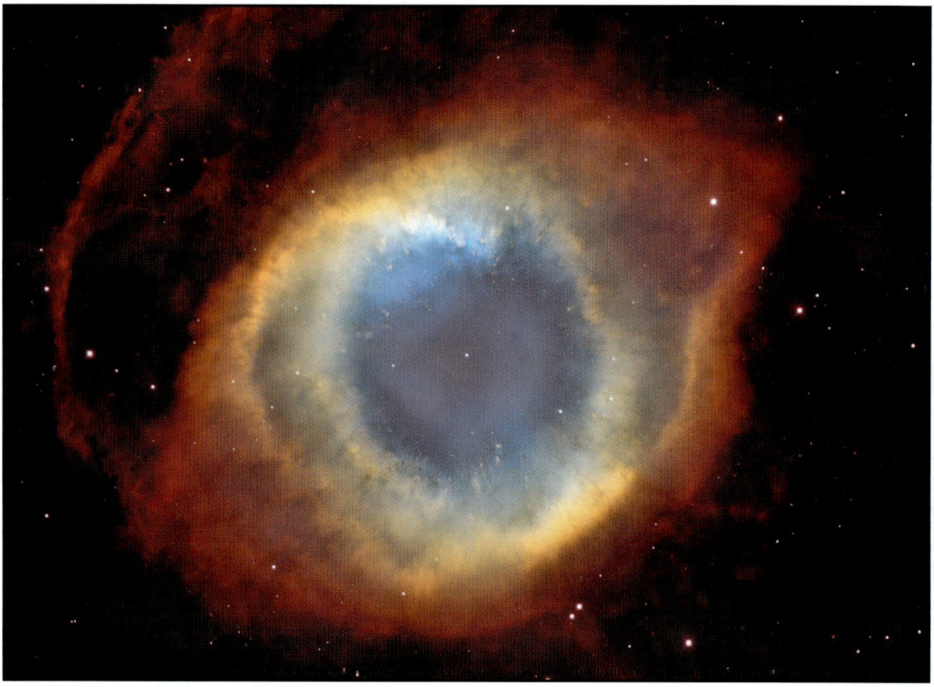

9. The "Eye of God" – The Hubble telescope captured a dying star that was named "The Eye of God" because it eerily appeared in the form of a large eye.

10. The "Crown of Thorns" – Captured by the Hubble telescope on the southern constellation Indus, a ghostly halo surrounded by cosmic dust forms what resembles a large crown of thorns!

11. The "Hand of God" – Another Hubble image captured the dust and gas that formed the image of a large hand which appears to cover a comet. This image was named the "Hand of God."

12. The "Destruction of the Tsunami" – As we enter the signs of the end times, Luke said that the "sea and the waves will be roaring, or agitated" (Luke 21:25-27). The tsunami reveals what can occur when the earth shakes under the sea.

Muslims fighting Hindus, the Hindus and Muslims fighting Christians, and so forth.

The natural birth process is divided into three trimesters. Months one to three are the first trimester. Months four to six represent the second trimester, and months seven to nine the third trimester. The most intense labor pains are experienced in the third trimester, close to the time of birth. There have been small birth pains throughout history, but the most intense are to occur just before the return of the Messiah.

War Signs and Birth Pains

I have heard Christians say, "Why do you believe we are in the time of the end? Haven't there always been famines, pestilences, earthquakes, wars, and other commotions on earth? What makes our generation any different from past generations?" The key is the phrase, "All of these." When all of these things begin to occur at the same time, then we are in the early seasons of the birth pains. If a person took the time to examine the records of famines, disease, and earthquakes during the past fifty years, they would see a huge increase in the activity of these three "signs," especially over the past few years, If war is considered to be a birth pain, we have seen many wars in the twentieth century that are certainly birth pain wars.

World War I lasted from 1914 to 1918. It was also called the "Great War," and the "War to End All Wars." The conflict mobilized more nations and armies than any other time in world history, producing the highest number of deaths (nine million) and injuries in history. War broke up the ruling families and monarchies of Europe and introduced Communism to the world through the Russian revolution. Millions of civilians were killed and injured, not only by the destruction of their businesses and homes, but by starvation and genocide initiated by invading armies. This war would impact even Israel.

During the war the British were running out of gun powder for their explosives. A Jewish chemist named Chaim Weizmann, director of the British Admiralty laboratories from 1916 to 1919, invented a way of mass producing acetone, which was a critical substance the allies used in the war. Without his assistance, some suggest the allies could have lost the war, or at least experienced major setbacks. In order to honor Weizmann's important contribution, British Foreign Secretary Arthur James Balfour presented a declaration to Lord Rothschild called the "Balfour Declaration." It expressed the wishes of the British Cabinet to establish a homeland in Palestine for the Jewish people. It read:

Foreign Office
November 2nd, 1917

Dear Lord Rothschild,

I have much pleasure in conveying to you, on behalf of His Majesty's Government, the following declaration of sympathy with Jewish Zionist aspirations which has been submitted to, and approved by the Cabinet: "His Majesty's Government view with favor the establishment in Palestine of a national home for the Jewish people, and will use their best endeavors to facilitate the achievement of this object, it being clearly understood that nothing shall be done which may prejudice the civil and religious right of existing non-Jewish communities in Palestine, or the rights and political status enjoyed by Jews in any other country." I should be grateful if you would bring this declaration to the knowledge of the Zionist Federation.

Yours sincerely,
Arthur James Balfour

While this declaration was an initial act to welcome Jews back to Palestine, the vast majority of Jews remained in Europe, continuing their businesses, raising their children, and building their homes. It would take more than a declaration to motivate hundreds of thousands of Jews to leave the prosperity of Europe and return to Palestine, a barren land of dry desert, rocks, and swamps.

It is often said that World War II was a continuation of World War I. The rise of Hitler and the Nazi Third Reich paved the road to the concentration camps where over six million Jews were exterminated. While in prison for eight months, Hitler wrote the first volume of his infamous book *Mein Kampf* (My Struggle), in which, among other things, he blamed the Jews for the world's problems; that is, for democracy, Communism, internationalism, and Germany's defeat in Word War I. The second edition of *Mein Kampf* was printed in 1927, and it gave instructions on how to conduct an uprising to exalt the Nazi Party. Five million copies were sold by the beginning of World War II.

After World War I the allies Britain, France, and America were demanding reparations from Germany. In order to punish Germany, the European banks began to devalue Germany's money. In 1919, the German mark traded at nine German marks for one American dollar. In 1920, it traded at sixty-five marks for one dollar, and two years later at 495 marks for one dollar. By 1923, the German mark traded for an incredible 18,000 marks for every dollar. Six months later the exchange was 350,000 marks per dollar, and one month after that, 4,620,000 marks per dollar. By November of 1923, the exchange was 4.2 trillion marks for one American dollar! The allies had effectively collapsed the German currency and banking system, and thus the German economy. Germans were left with worthless paper, and they were seen dumping wheelbarrows full of currency into bonfires. I have a stamp collection which includes German stamps printed during this time of hyperinflation. In the collection are a series of stamps from 1923, and on one small postage stamp the price indicates fifty-million German marks!

This hyperinflation in Germany created panic, poverty, and eventually a holocaust. It was the failure of the currency and the difficult economic times the German people encountered that created the perception that Jewish bankers were to blame and could have prevented the crisis. This banking conspiracy made it easier for Hitler to blame the Jews for both Germany's economic crisis and other world problems, such as the rise of Communism, which Hitler noted was a political concept started by a Jew named Karl Marx.

On November 29, 1947, following World War II and the holocaust, the United Nations voted by a narrow margin to partition Palestine and give the Jews access to form a state within the borders of Palestine. The U.S. President Harry Truman was at first hesitant to declare a new homeland for the Jewish people. But as the world began to see the mass graves, the ovens, and the showers where entire Jewish families were exterminated, a brief season of compassion came upon the people living in Canada, America, and Europe.

When Truman discussed the possibility of a Jewish state, he was heavily resisted by administration officials within our own government, especially in the State Department. Many in the Truman administration believed that the resistance of certain career men in the State Department was based upon anti-Semitism and not diplomacy. An older Jewish statesman named Chaim Weizmann, who served as president of national B'nai B'rith, attempted to make contact with Truman to ensure that he would support the new Jewish state. This was a turning point for Truman. After meeting with Weizmann, President Truman assured him that America would stand in support of the Jewish state.

Despite opposition from General Marshall and others in the State Department, all of whom feared a war with the Arabs, Truman kept his word. On May 13th, 1948, one of the President's cabinet members quoted Deuteronomy to Truman:

> "Behold. I have set the land before you: go in and possess the land which the Lord swear unto your fathers, Abraham, Isaac, and Jacob, to give them and to their seed after them."

Word came to the White House that on Friday, May 14th at midnight in Jerusalem a Jewish State would be announced. When the White House received the necessary papers to officially recognize the new Jewish State, the name of the country was left blank—because the name was unknown. When the announcement came through David Ben Gurion that the new state was named Israel, the American delegation at the United Nations broke out into laughter, thinking it was a joke. But it was no joke. The birth pains of the Second World War saw the fulfillment of the Balfour Declaration and a literal rebirth of Israel through the influence of Jews, including a chemist named Chaim Weizmann, for whom the Balfour Declaration was originally written in 1917. (Source: Truman Volume II, the Easton Press, Norwalk Conn., Collector's Edition, pages 600 – 621)

Two Types of Birth Pains

As with the natural birthing process, there are two types of labor pains: true and false pains. In the prophetic realm there are both true and false birth pains. I can recall several false labor pains during the past several years. In the late 1980s a man wrote a book which stirred interest in Christ's return. The book was called, "88 Reasons Why Jesus Will Return in 1988." The week before the predicted return of Christ, the attendance in the average church was up thirty percent and the altars were filled with seekers who wanted to ensure they would be prepared if the prediction came to pass. In 1989 the church remained, and another less popular book was written, indicating a one-year mistake in the calculation. But 1990 came, and the church remained.

In 1992 when Yasser Arafat, chairman of the Palestinian Liberation Organization, shook hands with Israeli Prime Minister Yitzhak Rabin on the lawn of the White House, the prophetic newsletters were burning up the presses. Some teachers announced that the seven-year treaty of Daniel 9:27 had now been signed. Some began projecting the seven- year tribulation and setting dates for the return of Christ. From 1992 to 1999 is seven years. Needless to say, this agreement was not the covenant of Daniel 9:27, and Yasser Arafat, was not the antichrist of Bible Prophecy. Again, a false pain was read as a real birthing sign.

The year 1999 brought a third false birth pain. The national media, influenced by computer experts, announced a possible global computer crash that was scheduled to change civilization on midnight, January 1, 2000. Speculation was that, since computer code involves ones and zeros, the internal clock in the computers might cause the system to completely shut down. By late 1999 grocery stores, survival supply houses, and computer centers were doing a booming business, as some projected that life as we knew it was about to change and set us back into the late 1800s. A surge of relief was felt when the media, spread throughout the nations of the world, showed live coverage of the New Year's Eve celebrations and we saw that the lights were still on and the computers were still working. Except for a few minor glitches, Y2K predictions proved to be a false labor pain.

The wars of the twentieth century, however, were a true birth pain that led to the rebirthing of Israel as a nation and the reunification of Jerusalem as the capital of Israel following the Six Day War in 1967.

What Should Believers Look For?

If we continue to read the Olivet Discourse and move beyond the wars and rumors of wars, there is one verse that is especially significant to all Christians:

> *"And this gospel of the kingdom shall be preached in all the world for a witness unto all nations; and then shall the end come."*
>
> —Matthew 24:14 (KJV)

From 32 AD, the suggested time of the birth of the church (Acts 2:1-4), to the destruction of Jerusalem and the Temple in 70 AD, is approximately thirty-eight years, or within one generation. During this time the Apostles and believers acted upon the great commission, to go into all parts of the world and preach the gospel to every person (Matthew 28:19-20). Some understood that the gospel would be preached among the nations and then the end would come. By 70 AD, the end came, but it was not the end of the age. Instead, it was the end of Israel as a Jewish nation, the end of Jerusalem, and the end of the Temple.

There is, however, a generation living at the time of the end that will also preach the gospel to the nations. The end, alluding to the conclusion of the dispensation of the grace of God (Ephesians 3:2), will climax with the return of Christ for the church, followed by the dreaded tribulation (Matthew 24:15). As believers who recognize the signs of the time of the end, we must alert ourselves to several important prophecies.

The Harvest is the End of the Age

In the parable of the wheat and tares, the Lord tells us that the harvest is the end of the age (Matthew 13:39). The harvest here indicates souls coming to Christ and does not refer to natural wheat or grain grown on a farm. James spoke of the harvest when writing:

> *"So be patient, brethren, [as you wait] till the coming of the Lord. See how the farmer waits expectantly for the precious harvest from the land. [See how] he keeps up his patient [vigil] over it until it receives the early and late rains. So you also must be patient. Establish your hearts [strengthen and confirm them in the final certainty], for the coming of the Lord is very near."*
>
> *–James 5:7-8 (AMP)*

In ancient Israel, the seven feasts were celebrated on or around the harvest and rain cycles. Passover was the first offering of the ripe barley and Pentecost centered on the wheat harvest. During the Feast of Tabernacles, God was honored for the seven fruits of the land. On the last day of the feast, a great water libation ceremony was conducted by the High Priest as prayers were offered for the winter rains to come and bless the land for the upcoming year's crops.

There is a beautiful picture of the harvest cycles and rain cycles of Israel, which tells us how they prophetically fit into the scenarios of the time of the end. James tells us that the farmer watched over the growth of his crops until he received the early and latter rain. In Scripture, natural rain is a picture of spiritual rain, or the outpouring of the Holy Spirit (Acts 2:17-18).

It is the preaching of the gospel to the nations and the outpouring of the Holy Spirit that will bring about the end time harvest which occurs at the end of the age. As the hearts of men ripen, then the Holy Spirit will move to reap a massive harvest from the field, as the laborers place their sickles into the golden grain. When we consider the harvest cycles, it is clear that the adversary is not content to sit idly by near the edge of the field and watch the harvesters gather in the souls into the master's house. There is a pattern found in the Scriptures that battles erupt during harvest time!

- Sampson's battles occurred during the wheat harvest — Judges 15:1

- Gideon's battles occurred during the wheat harvest — Judges 6:11

- The Ark judgment happened during the wheat harvest — 1 Samuel 6:13

- David's battles happened during harvest time — 2 Samuel 4:6

- Rizpah lost her sons during the barley harvest — 2 Samuel 21:9

In Matthew 13:24-30, Christ gave a parable of a farmer planting seed to produce good wheat. On one occasion while he was sleeping, an enemy came and secretly planted seed into the ground. When the harvest ripened, the farmer noticed there were dark tares scattered throughout the field. The danger of a tare is that, if you attempt to pull it from the ground, you will also pull a clump of wheat up with it, as the roots of the tare are interwoven with the roots of the wheat. Thus, good wheat will be damaged in the process.

Jesus revealed that the wheat and tares would grow together until the final harvest:

> *"Let both grow together until the harvest: and in the time of harvest I will say to the reapers, Gather ye together first the tares, and bind them in bundles to burn them: but gather the wheat into my barn."* — Matthew 13:24-30 (KJV)

The wheat represents the children of the Kingdom of God and the tares are those who are a part of Satan's kingdom (Matthew 13:38). I believe the parable can allude to people who will come in the name of Christ and deceive others (Matthew 24:5). They will plant false doctrine into the church. Recently some strange, heretical teaching has surfaced in the Body of Christ that corrupts and counters the sound doctrine of Scripture and the teachings of the first century saints. The tares are removed by God Himself who sends his angels (messengers) to sever the righteous from the unjust (Matthew 13:41).

A Hidden Message in the Parables

The four gospels record many of the parables of Christ. There are, among those parables, several key stories whose theme centers on the return of Christ; among them are the parable of the ten virgins (Matthew 25:1-13) and the parable of the King's son's wedding (Matthew 22:2-14). There are three specific parables recorded in Luke 15:4-32 that I believe give an important insight into the battles that believers will encounter at the time of the end. They are the parable of the lost son (Luke 15:11-32), the woman with the lost coin (Luke 15:8-9), and the shepherd with the lost sheep (Luke 15:4-7).

In the first parable the father had two sons. One had a wild streak, and he took his future inheritance from his father and went into a far country to live recklessly. He ended up living on a farm and feeding pigs. Once he came to his senses, he returned back home where this prodigal son received a welcome equal to a king!

In the next parable, a woman had ten coins and lost one. In Christ's time, a woman would often wear some of her husband's wealth in a necklace around her neck. In this case, she did not lose just any coin; she lost a coin that was important to her husband and her family. She searched through the entire house and eventually discovered the lost coin.

The third parable in the series involved a shepherd. He had one hundred sheep and discovered that one was missing. At night the shepherds in ancient Israel brought their sheep into a cave. Each shepherd would hold his rod just above the head of the sheep and count them to ensure that all sheep were safe. At some point the shepherd discovered that one of his sheep was missing. Without a shepherd, the little sheep could be killed by a bear, a lion, or a wolf. He immediately left his sheep in the safekeeping of another shepherd and went on a search for the one lost sheep.

In all three parables, the individual lost something: a son, a coin, and a sheep. In each case, that which was lost either returned or was found; and in all three instances there was rejoicing over the return of that which was lost.

I believe these three parables reveal clues as to the types of attacks we as believers will experience in the time of the end:

- There will be attacks against our children;
- There will be attacks against our family finances;
- There will be attacks in the church, with sheep missing from God's house.

During prophetic seasons there have always been assaults against the infants and children. In Egypt, Pharaoh demanded that all sons born to the Hebrews be thrown into the Nile River. Herod instructed the Roman soldiers to slay all infants in and around Bethlehem who were under two years of age. In our generation, our sons and daughters are being tempted to take drugs, drink alcohol, become promiscuous, and question the Christian faith in which they were raised. At times they leave our protection and are pulled into the bright lights of the city, like an insect attracted to porch lights at night. We must pray for their protection and believe God to bring them home, claiming the promise that if we train them up in the way they should go, they will not depart from it but will eventually return!

There is definitely an attack on family finances. The woman had ten coins but lost one. One coin out of ten is the tenth, or the tithe. Her "tithe" was missing. With the economic downturn, I often hear ministers tell me that people are cutting back on their giving, especially their tithe. I was always taught, and still believe, that the tithe did not belong to me but belonged to the Lord. It would have been easy for the woman to say, "Oh well, I don't know what happened but there's nothing I can do about it." Instead, she went to work to get back what was missing. We as believers can become too passive in our attitude when the adversary comes against our finances. Instead of accepting what is happening, we must get the broom out and start sweeping. Begin to pursue our dream and vision, until we get back whatever the enemy is attempting to steal.

The story of the shepherd and the lost sheep is also practical for our generation. Those who faithfully attend church are aware of how easy it is for some to stop attending church. They are missing from the service; yet, weeks or months might pass before someone expresses concern for their well being. I once heard a man say, "When I was a sinner I could not beat the Christians away as they all tried to convert me. When I had family problems with my wife and she left me, I could not find any of those Christians anywhere near me!" We as believers should watch each other's backs. When we see a fellow sheep faltering or in danger, we should step in to do whatever is necessary to restore the lost sheep. If we refuse, then the wild beasts (unsaved men) and wolves (people who devourer others) will destroy a member of the flock.

We need to be aware of the end-time attacks that believers will experience in the last days, and be prepared to take action accordingly. We must also remember that our end-time assignment is to fulfill the great commission to preach the gospel, teach all nations, and baptize in water all who receive the gospel of Jesus Christ.

CHAPTER 6

The Sign of the Son of Man in Heaven

"And there shall be signs in the sun and in the moon, and in the stars; and upon the earth distress of nations, with perplexity; the sea and the waves roaring;

Men's hearts failing them for fear, and for looking after those things which are coming on the earth: for the powers of heaven shall be shaken.

"And then shall they see the Son of man coming in a cloud with power and great glory, and when these things begin to come to pass, then look up, and lift up your heads; for your redemption draweth nigh." —Luke 21:25-28 (KJV)

Several years ago I was pouring over the prophecies found in Matthew 24, Mark 13, and Luke 21. As I observed the difference in the wording of the prophecies in all the gospels, it seemed that Luke brought out certain details that are not emphasized by Matthew or Mark. I was intrigued by how it seemed that Christ actually gave an order of events recorded in Luke's gospel. He begins with cosmic signs and concludes with His appearing to redeem His people.

When reading the order of events, they are as follows:

- The sun
- The moon
- The stars
- National distress
- Sea and waves
- Powers of heaven

During the twentieth century, astronomers and scientists began to observe the sun in a manner that would have been impossible in Christ's time. There was a very strange "sign" on the moon in 1969, when the spacecraft Apollo landed on the moon surface, transmitting back to earth Man's first walk on the moon. This was certainly an amazing feat that I would suggest is also a cosmic sign, or a sign on the moon, as alluded to by Christ.

During the 1990s there was, what I would consider to be, a remarkable sign among the stars in the heavens. We have all heard of Halley's Comet, which can be seen from earth about every seventy-five to seventy-eight years. It was first seen by astronomers in 240 BC and was last seen in our inner Solar System in 1986. Halley's Comet was named after Edmond Halley (1656-1742), a close friend of Sir Isaac Newton. Halley researched twenty-five comets and discovered they all had predictable paths.

The comet was observed in October of 12 BC, the same time that Herod the Great was expanding the Jewish Temple in Jerusalem. The same comet then reappeared between seventy-seven and seventy-eight years later over Jerusalem in 66 AD, when a series of strange signs began to occur over the city of Jerusalem. The Jewish historian Josephus records:

"There was a star resembling a sword, which stood over the city, and a comet that continued a whole year…on the eighth day of the month of Nissan and at the ninth hour of the night, so great a light shone around the altar and the holy house that it appeared to be bright daytime; which light lasted half an hour…"

– *Josephus*, War of the Jews, Book VI,

This comet might have been the same that is mentioned in the Jewish Talmud as "a star which appears once in seventy years that makes the captains of the ships err" (source: The Talmud Harioth, Chapter III). The comet appeared in April, 1910 and reappeared in February, 1986. The 66 AD, 1910, and 1986 dates are unique because of events that followed.

Four years after the 66 AD appearance, the Roman legions surrounded Jerusalem, invaded the city, and destroyed the Temple. Four years following the 1910 sighting, World War II erupted. At the conclusion, the Balfour Declaration was signed, giving the Jewish people access to live in Palestine. Slightly over four years following the Halley's sighting in 1986, the Gulf War ensued and Saddam Hussein shot scud missiles into Israel as he attempted to pull Israel into the war.

On April 24, 1061, Halley's Comet sparked a monk to announce that the country would be destroyed. In the year 1066, there was an outbreak of wars that included the Battle of Fulford, (Norway and British militia), the Battle of Stamford, and the Battle of Hastings, when William the Conqueror invaded and conquered England.

In our own generation, one of the largest and most magnificent comets passed through our solar system. Named the Hale-Bopp comet, it was first spotted April 27, 1993, which on the Hebrew calendar was the forty-fifth-year anniversary of the British mandate that ended Palestine and rebirthed Israel as a nation. On July 23, 1995, the comet was spotted in the constellation called Sagittarius, the half-beast half-man that some suggest pictures the coming antichrist. It was reported that this comet was last seen 4,200 years ago, at the same time when Noah was constructing the Ark. This large comet, which is 50,000 times brighter than Halley's Comet, exited the galaxy on the Jewish Feast of Pentecost through the constellation Orion.

Just as Halley's Comet sometimes passed by about four years before a conflict among the nations, the Hale-Bopp Comet came through slightly fewer than four years before September 11, 2001, the date which initiated a global war on terror.

It appears that comets are linked to a sign of coming conflict. In many instances the battles occur within four to six years after the comet's appearance. Jewish sages have many commentaries related to comets.

Shaking in the Heavens

There is coming a seven-year timeframe identified as the "great tribulation" in Matthew 24:21 and Revelation 7:14. The many judgments that strike the earth are the results of an apocalyptic shaking in the heavens. Several Biblical prophets wrote about these days when they said:

> *"Behold, the day of the LORD comes, cruel, with both wrath and fierce anger, to lay the land desolate; and He will destroy its sinners from it. For the stars of heaven and their constellations will not give their light; the sun will be darkened in its going forth, and the moon will not cause its light to shine."* —Isaiah 13:9-10

> *"Therefore I will shake the heavens, and the earth will move out of her place, in the wrath of the LORD of hosts and in the day of His fierce anger."* — Isaiah 13:13

> *""For thus says the LORD of hosts: 'Once more (it is a little while) I will shake heaven and earth, the sea and dry land."* — Haggai 2:6

The future shaking of the earth and heavens will be the result of falling stars and a large asteroid striking the earth. This was seen by the Apostle John in the book of Revelation.

> *"And the third angel sounded, and there fell a great star from heaven, burning as it were a lamp, and it fell upon the third part of the rivers, and upon the fountains of waters; And the name of the star is called Wormwood: and the third part of the waters became wormwood; and many men died of the waters, because they were made bitter."* — Revelation 8:10-11

The Greek word for great in Revelation 8:10 means, "exceedingly great, large and mighty." This is not a small falling star that can barely be seen from earth in the darkness of the night. It is a very large star that falls to the earth. This word star is *aster,* the same word used by Christ in Matthew 24:29 and Mark 13:25. It is used throughout the book of Revelation to warn of falling stars during the tribulation. The English word asteroid is derived from the word aster. This great star is an asteroid that "burns like a lamp." This phrase identifies what the asteroid looks like to those dwelling on earth. It not only describes the glow in the heavens, but the tail of the asteroid that is following the falling star. In Luke's gospel he speaks of signs in the stars (Luke 21:25). The word here for stars is astron, the root word for the English word astronomy.

When this asteroid eventually strikes the earth, it will produce many of the judgments and terrible events predicted in the book of Revelation. In June of 1908, near the Tunguska River in Russia, a mysterious event took place that is still being examined to this day. A massive explosion took place about three to six miles above the earth's surface that blew trees to the ground for one thousand square miles. Modern researchers who believe in UFO's believe this was the result of a UFO landing in Siberia. Scientists, however, identify this as the breakup of a comet or a meteorite, whose impact on the earth was so great that it literally knocked the surrounding forest to the ground.

When the future apocalyptic asteroid enters the earth's atmosphere, it will create much of the havoc predicted by John in the book of Revelation, and also by Christ:

> *"But in those days, after that tribulation, the sun shall be darkened, and the moon shall not give her light, And the stars of heaven shall fall, and the powers that are in heaven shall be shaken."*
>
> —Mark 13:24-25 (KJV)

> *"And the stars of heaven fell unto the earth, even as a fig tree casteth her untimely figs, when she is shaken of a mighty wind. And the heaven departed as a scroll when it is rolled together; and every mountain and island were moved out of their places."*
>
> —Revelation 6:13-14 (KJV)

Several years ago I was watching a major documentary on asteroids. The commentator was detailing what would follow in America if a sizeable asteroid struck the edge of Mexico. After the large comet or meteorite struck the waters off the coasts, immediately a tsunami with twenty-foot-high waves moving at five hundred miles per hour would move to the coastline of the United States, affecting every coastal city in the Gulf of Mexico. It would wipe out everything on the coasts and then travel inland for about fifty miles. All ships, including cruise ships, fishing vessels, and military battleships would be overturned and destroyed.

The falling star would heat the atmosphere 280 degrees, and the impact would send hot metal up, which would reheat the atmosphere and send bits of the hot star raining back down. Scientists say the land temperature on earth would raise the normal temperature from about seventy-five degrees to as high as seven hundred degrees! The only survivors would be those who could take shelter in deep underground chambers and caverns, and remain there until the ground cools and the dust settles. The particles from the debris would cover the earth and darken the light of the sun for many weeks or several months. Finally, the food supply in surrounding areas would be devastated, thus creating famine and food shortages.

It's All in the Apocalypse

When we compare the above information to what we read in the book of Revelation, it is clear that the coming asteroid will fulfill many of the predicted judgments coming to earth in the future.

After this asteroid strikes the earth, we read of a series of terrible events that immediately follow. First we read of the destruction of ships. John wrote, *"A third of the sea creatures and a third of the ships were destroyed..."* (Revelation 8:9). About 70.8% of the earth is covered by water, with 29.2% being different forms of land, including mountains, deserts and plains. Only the impact of an asteroid, producing a massive tsunami, could destroy a third of the water, sea creatures, and ships. This appears to occur in one specific area of the world.

We read where the drinking waters become polluted; *"A third of the rivers and fountains made bitter..."* (Revelation 8:10-11). During both a volcanic eruption and the strike of a meteorite, the water becomes acidic and undrinkable. An asteroid could cause the pH balance in the water to change, thus making the waters bitter. The star will be named wormwood, which means *bitterness* (Revelation 8:11). The word wormwood is found in passages in the Old Testament as well.

In ancient Jerusalem there were many cisterns carved from limestone that were used to store rainwater. In ancient times there was one main water source that also provided drinking water for the city, and that was the Gihon Spring. The water originated from an underground source and surfaced at a large, flowing spring. During the end of David's reign, the High Priest Zadok led David's young son Solomon on the king's donkey and anointed him with oil at the pool of Siloam.

In the years 1016, 1033, and 1066 AD there were a series of earthquakes that struck Jerusalem. During the 1066 quake, twenty-five thousand lives were lost and only two houses remained (Source: The History of the Jews in the Latin Kingdom of Jerusalem; Claredon, Oxford Press, page 15). After the 1066 quake, the Academy of the Jews was moved from Jerusalem to the city of Tyre, Lebanon. When a major quake occurs, it can have an effect on the underground springs. It appears something happened to the Gihon Springs in the time of Jeremiah:

> *"Therefore thus saith the LORD of hosts, the God of Israel; Behold, I will feed them, even this people, with wormwood, and give them water of gall to drink."* —Jeremiah 9:15 (KJV)

> *"Therefore thus saith the LORD of hosts concerning the prophets; Behold, I will feed them with wormwood, and make them drink the water of gall: for from the prophets of Jerusalem is profaneness gone forth into all the land."* —Jeremiah 23:15 (KJV)

Speaking in terms of symbolism, Jeremiah was telling the Jews that they had been enjoying the waters of the Gihon, but because of their iniquity and perversion, they were going to drink from bitter waters. He called these waters wormwood. That same word is used in the apocalypse to identify the condition of the drinking water after the asteroid hits.

The next verse in Revelation mentions the impact on the sun and moon as, *"A third of the sun and moon were darkened…"* (Revelation 8:12). A large dust cloud would cover the atmosphere and create total darkness; thus, the sun would appear to be darkened. This judgment would again be linked to the fallout of the asteroid. We are informed in Revelation 8:7 that *"Hail, fire, and blood were cast upon the earth…"* This results in the destruction of one third of the grass and trees as they are burned. This could be caused by the hot metal shooting back into the atmosphere and raining down on earth, burning up every green plant within range of the debris. Notice that John saw one third of everything—the sea, sea creatures, ships, rivers, grass, and trees—being affected.

> Later in Revelation we read where there is a great heat released on the earth: "And men were scorched with great heat, and blasphemed the name of God, which hath power over these plagues: and they repented not to give him glory."
>
> —Revelation 16:9 (KJV)

The prophet Isaiah alluded to this event when he wrote:

> "Moreover the light of the moon shall be as the light of the sun, and the light of the sun shall be sevenfold, as the light of seven days, in the day that the LORD bindeth up the breach of his people, and healeth the stroke of their wound.
>
> "Behold, the name of the LORD cometh from far, burning with his anger, and the burden thereof is heavy: his lips are full of indignation, and his tongue as a devouring fire."
>
> —Isaiah 30:26-27 (KJV)

If the normal temperature in a region is seventy degrees, then seven times hotter would be 490 degrees. In my early ministry I thought the sun would heat up and impact the entire earth. The main challenge to this idea is that, if the temperature was double, it would shut down all power grids. In a short time, not just a third, but everything on earth would die. However, an asteroid would increase the level of heat in the atmosphere and on the ground. Thus again, these strange prophecies can be fulfilled with the strike of a destructive asteroid.

One of the more unusual predictions is found in Isaiah:

> "Therefore I will shake the heavens, and the earth shall remove out

of her place, in the wrath of the LORD of hosts, and in the day of his fierce anger." —Isaiah 13:13 (KJV)

The earth moves with its axis pointing toward the North Star. During the tsunami of 2004, not only did the plates under the Indian Ocean shift, causing a deadly tsunami, but it slightly impacted the rotation of the earth. It shifted slightly on its axis, though not enough to create any damage to the planet. A large asteroid, however, could cause the earth to be moved out of place.

People will Run to the Mountains

When such devastation spreads like a dust storm over the earth, what will men do? Several years ago I traveled to Greenbrier, West Virginia for a complete physical at their clinic. During our stay, my son Jonathan and I toured a secret bunker that was constructed from 1959 to 1962, while the Resort Hotel was expanding its guest rooms and constructing a diagnostic clinic. The bunker was built in the event of a nuclear attack on the nation's capital. There were large tunnels to store food, dormitories for sleeping, a hospital, a kitchen, and a cafeteria that seated four hundred people. The site had a decontamination area, underground diesel generators, an underground water filtering system with three holding tanks capable of storing 25,000 gallons of water each, and even a place to burn garbage and, yes, dead bodies, if a person died while inside the bunker. There were special meeting auditoriums for the Congress and Senate, and a large convention center that would serve as the offices of the legislative branch of government in the event of a national nuclear crisis.

At any given time there were between twelve and fifteen government employees working twenty-four hours a day, in and around the hotel, to ensure the security of the bunker. There was even a railway station next to the hotel where the legislative branch would be brought by rail, if necessary.

After thirty-five years, the secrecy of the bunker was broken in May of 1992 when the Washington Post printed a story. A reporter was investigating a company that had government contracts, but was in financial crisis. The reporter obtained information showing that two very large steel doors had been delivered to the Greenbrier Hotel, in West Virginia. This led to many questions and eventually the secret hideaway being exposed to the nation.

Most every government in the world has certain secret locations underground, where their leaders can hide and operate the government from underground facilities. Presently some bunkers in America that have served in the past as storage arsenals for weapons, are being converted into both living quarters and food storage facilities. As one friend said to me, "We prepare bunkers for what the next war will be fought over, and in the future it will be over food and food shortages."

If an announcement were made that an asteroid was headed to earth and there were only seventy-two hours to prepare, then what we read in Revelation 6:15-16 would become a reality:

> "And the kings of the earth, and the great men, and the rich men, and the chief captains, and the mighty men, and every bondman, and every free man, hid themselves in the dens and in the rocks of the mountains; "And said to the mountains and rocks, Fall on us, and

hide us from the face of him that sitteth on the throne, and from the wrath of the Lamb." —Revelation 6:15-16 (JKV)

Notice the phrase *rocks of the mountains* and the word *dens*. In the New Testament there are two Greek words used for caves and dens. A Greek word for caves is *ope*, and it is used in Hebrews 11:38, where the righteous men lived in dens and caves. This word often refers to a hole or opening in the rocks, such as a small cave. The Greek word *spelaion* is the word for dens in Revelation 6:15. It is also used in John 11:38 to indicate the grave where Lazarus was laid, as ancient Roman tombs were cut into limestone rocks. The dens can be manmade bunkers and underground tunnels prepared in the event of national crisis and nuclear war.

The announcement of an approaching asteroid would send people from entire nations running for cover into bunkers, tunnels, and underground chambers. Those in the mountains will begin praying for the rocks to fall on them and hide or kill them. People are terrified, knowing what is coming to the earth. Christ warned that men's hearts would fail them for fear, and for looking after those things which are coming to pass upon the earth. He warned that the powers of heaven will be shaken (Luke 21:26).

The Powers of Heaven Shaken

In the warning, "the powers of heaven will be shaken," the Greek word for heaven is the words *ouranos*, from which we derive our word uranium. The Greek word for powers is *dunamis*, which is an explosive type of power. Our English word is dynamite. The third important word is *shaken*. The Greek word for shaken alludes to something being shaken out of its place or moved off balance. If we were to reword that phrase using the Greek meaning of the words, the phrase could read, "the explosive power of uranium will shake things out of their place."

Uranium is a key substance of nuclear weapons. When the Hebrew prophets were receiving visions of the time of the end, and when John recorded the apocalypse, there were no weapons of mass destruction on earth. In those days, cities were overrun by armies and burned with fire. These fires would burn for days.

In Revelation 18, John recorded the destruction of the city called "mystery Babylon." He saw that Babylon was drunk with the blood of the saints and martyrs of Christ (Revelation 17:6). It is clear that John was alluding to Rome, Italy where Imperial Rome was persecuting and killing Christians. Paul had already been beheaded in Rome, and the Christians in John's day were in hiding for fear of death. In John's time, it was common to veil the name of Rome by using the name Babylon, since both Babylon and Rome had invaded Israel, destroyed Jerusalem, razed and destroyed the Jewish Temple, and carried Jews captive to Babylon and Rome. Thus, ancient Babylon was a picture of Rome in John's time.

When John saw this city being destroyed, he mentioned three times that the city was destroyed in one hour (Revelation 18:10, 17 and 19). In John's time it would have been impossible to destroy a city the size of Rome in one hour. In fact, in 64 AD when Nero was accused of burning Rome, the fire started at shops clustered around the Circus Maximus and burned for six days and seven nights. According to the writings of Tacitus, the fire destroyed four of fourteen districts and damaged seven others. According to a letter Seneca sent to Paul, there were one hundred-thirty-two houses and four blocks that were burned in six days; the seventh brought a pause.

The point is, about ten percent of Rome burned for almost seven days in 64 AD. In John's vision the future city identified with Mystery Babylon will be destroyed in one hour:

"The kings of the earth who committed fornication and lived luxuriously with her will weep and lament for her, when they see the smoke of her burning, standing at a distance for fear of her torment, saying, 'Alas, alas, that great city Babylon, that mighty city! For in one hour your judgment has come." – Revelation 18:9-10

John said the city will be destroyed in one hour and people will stand at a distance for fear of the torment, and because of the burning smoke (Revelation 18:9 and 18). The combination of three phrases, "in one hour, the smoke, and standing at a distance," could have reference to a nuclear blast that most likely would destroy an entire city in one hour. The fear of the smoke would be the fear of the radiation cloud moving through the atmosphere. This would make people stand at a distance, or as the King James translations says, "afar off."

Another danger that presents itself in our generation is the EMP, or the electromagnetic pulse bomb. Here is a description of this particular bomb:

"The general idea of an EMP is that it wrecks havoc on electronics, but leaves other physical structures mostly untouched. Real-life electromagnetic pulses released by high-altitude nuclear tests have fused power wires, triggered burglar alarms, and caused breakage of radios, televisions, and power lines as far away as 1,500 kilometers (930 miles). The source of the disruption is a large-scale, intensely fluctuating magnetic field created when high energy photons from an explosion knock electrons from their atomic orbit. This disruption becomes trapped within the earth's magnetic field, leading to a coherent oscillating electric current." (source: www.wisegeek.com/what-is-an-emp)

I once asked a friend in the U.S. military who deals with counter terrorism, what would occur in the event of an EMP bomb striking a large American city. His response was that it would burn up all copper wiring, so that objects such as lights, computers, electricity, and so forth would no longer work. The city would be set back to the way life was in the 1800s! The radial distance that would be affected would depend on certain factors, such as the vertical atmospheric distance of the blast.

In the Biblical prophecies concerning the wars that occur in the time of the end, I have always been curious as to why men are on horseback. Horses and riders are mentioned in the coming war of Gog and Magog, as well as in the future seven-year tribulation:

> "I will turn you around, put hooks into your jaws, and lead you out, with all your army, horses, and horsemen, all splendidly clothed, a great company with bucklers and shields, all of them handling swords. Persia, Ethiopia, and Libya are with them, all of them with shield and helmet" —Ezekiel 38:4-6

> "And thus I saw the horses in the vision: those who sat on them had breastplates of fiery red, hyacinth blue, and sulfur yellow; and the heads of the horses were like the heads of lions; and out of their mouths came fire, smoke, and brimstone." —Revelation 9:17

Many scholars suggest that John would have known nothing about modern warfare and, when revealing end time conflicts and wars, he would have simply identified with armies and weapons that were familiar to him in his time. While it is purely speculation, it may be possible that the "shaking of the heavens" is more than just cosmic activity such as falling stars, comets, or asteroids striking the planet. The shaking may also—and likely will include—nuclear weapons and electromagnetic pulse weapons that will destroy the power grids in modern nations and send the military back to the old fashioned way of fighting battles.

When we consider the deadly, destructive power of nuclear weapons, we can understand why the future tribulation "shall be a time of trouble, such as never was since there was a nation even to that same time" (Daniel 12:1), and "except those days be shortened there shall be no flesh saved." (Matthew 24:22).

Another Interpretation of the Powers of Heaven

When Christ predicted that the "powers of heaven would be shaken," there can be another interpretation. Most immediately think of the sun, moon, and stars. They are correct, in that these greater and lesser lights are heavenly powers, for without the sun all living things would die, and without the moon there would be a disruption in the tides of the ocean. There is, however, another form of power in the heavens, and that is the strength and force of violent winds. When watching the news following a major hurricane, it is shocking to see how trees are plucked up like toothpicks and large homes are turned into firewood. Jesus said the powers of heaven would be *shaken*. The Greek word means, *to waver, agitate, disturb,* and *to shake up*. The root word for *shaken* comes from the word *salos,* which means *a vibration* or *a wave*.

Christ predicted that the "sea and the waves would be roaring" prior to His return (Luke 21). There are two primary ways in which the sea and the waves are impacted. One is by a tsunami that slams destructive waves onto the coastlines of nations in the strike zone, and the other is by hurricane winds that bring rain and waves crashing into coastal areas. In the past few years, we have seen a major tsunami that impacted thirteen nations and killed and wounded hundreds of thousands of people. We have witnessed the devastation of New Orleans, Louisiana and Galveston, Texas, as well as smaller towns in various states. There seems to be an increase in the number of storms and their levels of destruction, not just with hurricanes but also tornadoes.

If we look back at the predictions of Christ in Luke, He gives an order that climaxes with the shaking of the powers of heaven (Luke 21:24-26):

1. the Gentiles lose grip on Jerusalem
2. signs in the sun
3. signs in the moon
4. signs in the stars
5. the shaking of the heavens

We have begun to see the fulfillment of these signs in our generation. After over 1900 years of being under control of Gentile powers—from the Romans to the British—Jerusalem once again became the capital of Israel in 1967. Today the Gentile nations no longer have total dominion over the city. We have seen men landing on the moon. We witnessed the comets, which indicated signs in the stars. Following the predictions, it seems that the next sign we will begin to see is a shaking of the heavens.

CHAPTER 7

The Sign of the Coming of the Son of Man

"What will be the sign of your coming and of the end of the world…" —Matthew 24:3 (KJV)

"Immediately after the tribulation of those days shall the sun be darkened, and the moon shall not give her light, and the stars shall fall from heaven, and the powers of the heavens shall be shaken: And then shall appear the sign of the Son of man in heaven: and then shall all the tribes of the earth mourn, and they shall see the Son of man coming in the clouds of heaven with power and great glory." —Matthew 24:29-30 (KJV)

The Greeks sought after wisdom, but the Jews required a sign (1 Corinthians 1:22). The priest Zacharias was burning incense at the golden altar when Gabriel appeared and predicted that his barren wife would conceive a son named John, who would come in the spirit of Elijah and prepare the way for the Lord (Luke 1:8-13). The older man must have forgotten about the miracle of Abraham and Sarah, because he questioned how it could be possible since they both were too old to have children. As any religious Jew would have required, he demanded a sign to prove that the angel's words were true. In anger, the angel struck him silent for nine months (Luke 1:18-19).

Jesus was continually confronted by sign seeking Pharisees who were looking for a specific, visible sign that He was the Messiah. We read:

> *"Then some of the scribes and Pharisees answered, saying, 'Teacher, we want to see a sign from You.' But He answered and said to them, "An evil and adulterous generation seeks after a sign, and no sign will be given to it except the sign of the prophet Jonah. For as Jonah was three days and three nights in the belly of the great fish, so will the Son of Man be three days and three nights in the heart of the earth."*
>
> —Matthew 12:38-40

Apparently, multiplying bread and fish and feeding five thousand men, healing every form of sickness, casting evil spirits from those who were possessed, and raising the dead were not enough evidence to convince these skeptical religious hypocrites (Matthew 23:13-15). On one occasion, Christ's own disciples began asking about a specific sign to indicate the visible proof of His return. Jesus said:

> *"And then shall appear the sign of the Son of man in heaven: and then shall all the tribes of the earth mourn, and they shall see the Son of man coming in the clouds of heaven with power and great glory."*
>
> —Matthew 24:30 (KJV)

If Jesus was the Messiah, why does He use the term, "Son of man," which is terminology used 108 times in the English translation of the Old Testament? When naming a son, it was a custom among the Jews to include the name of the father. In Hebrew, the word son is *ben,* and in the New Testament Greek and Aramiac the word *bar* is used. When alluding to the two Messiahs in Judaism, one is called Messiah ben Joseph and the other Messiah ben David. Translated into English they are the Messiah son of (ben) Joseph and Messiah son of (ben) David. In the New Testament there are names such as Simeon Bar-Jonah (Matthew 16:17) and Bartimaeus (Mark 10:46). These are not their last names, but instead mean, Simon son of Jonah and son of Timaeus. The term son of man was used by the prophets when speaking of themselves, or when God was addressing them, or commanding them to prophesy to the people. Out of the 108 uses of the term in the Old Testament, it is used differently in one place — the book of Daniel:

> *"I was watching in the night visions, and behold, one like the Son of Man, coming with the clouds of heaven! He came to the Ancient of Days, and they brought Him near before Him. Then to Him was given dominion and glory and a kingdom, that all peoples, nations, and languages should serve Him. His dominion is an everlasting dominion, which shall not pass away, and His kingdom the one which shall not be destroyed."* – Daniel 7:13-14

Jesus continually identified himself as the "Son of man." However, those who understood the Messianic prophecy penned by Daniel knew well that this term "Son of man" would also be used to identify the Messiah of Israel, who would come in the clouds and set up His everlasting kingdom in Jerusalem.

In Matthew 24, the wording that Jesus did *not* use is as significant as the wording He *did* use. Notice that He did not say, "Then you will see the Son of man in heaven." They asked for a single sign of His coming; and yet, Jesus began to list many signs, such as wars, famines, pestilence, earthquakes, and so on. He said that the gospel would be preached in the entire world as a witness to all nations; then He spoke of the tribulation. Jesus mentioned cosmic disorders in verse 29 that are parallel to the apocalyptic vision John saw over sixty years later. After all of this, Jesus said, "Then will appear the sign of the Son of man in heaven…."

What does that statement mean? Does it simply mean that the people will see Christ as He is returning, or is there a specific cosmic sign in the heavens that will indicate He is returning to earth?

What is the Sign of the Son of Man?

In the first years of the early church, an Aramaic word was coined that some believe was used to secretly identify Christians—the word Maranatha. It is found one place in the New Testament, where we read, "If any man love not the Lord Jesus Christ, let him be Anathema Maranatha" (1 Corinthians 16:22).

The word Anathema means accursed, but the word Maranatha is the Greek combination of two Aramaic words: *Maran*, meaning *Lord*, and *atha*, meaning *has come*. The complete word means "Our Lord has come." Modern translators say it means, "Our Lord cometh," while some Aramaic scholars regard the meaning as "O Lord come," a statement made by Paul expressing his desire for Christ's return.

In the Christian faith, there is one word that is universally recognized by all believers, and that is the word Hallelujah, which in Hebrew means "Praise ye the Lord." This one word can be spoken from a pulpit during a worldwide Christian convention where many people groups are unable to communicate with one another; yet each nation represented understands the word and its meaning. This one word is spoken in heaven, after the destruction of Babylon (Revelation 19:1, 3, 4, and 6).

When pondering the question, "What is the sign of the Son of man?" we might say that to Christians, one sign of Christ is the sign of the cross. Many years ago I toured the catacombs in Rome, Italy. The catacombs are miles of underground tunnels and burial places that were hidden under Rome, where many of the early Christians fled from persecution and secretly buried their dead. There are different types of carvings above the tombs, including doves, which represent the Holy Spirit, and whales, which represent the sign of Jonah that Christ gave the scribes and Pharisees. Jonah's body was preserved for three days and nights in the belly of a fish, and afterward he was brought out alive to warn Nineveh. The whale carvings were a sign that the person buried in the tomb was a Christian who anticipated a resurrection from the dead.

The Cross—An Early Emblem

The emblem of a cross did not originate with the Christian faith. It is one of the oldest and earliest symbols on earth, and it is used in many different world religions. For example, the Ankh use a cross-like symbol that is linked to the ancient Egyptians. The cross may have been used as far back as the time of Cain as a symbol of protection. When Cain slew Abel, God placed a mark on Cain's head to identify him and secure him from being hunted and killed (Genesis 4:15). The word "mark" in Genesis 4 is *owth* in Hebrew, and it indicates a sign or a token. The early Hebrew alphabet used symbols that later became letters of the alphabet.

The first letter, alef, was the symbol of an ox's head and the last letter, tav, was the symbol of a + or an x sign in the form of what we call a cross.

On September 19, 1991, two Austrians were hiking on the South Tyrolean Alps in Italy when they made a fascinating discovery. Helmet Simon spotted a body under the ice. Thinking perhaps it was a skier who had died in an avalanche years ago, they were stunned when the body was removed and dated as a man who had been killed in 3300 BC. This would date him, in Biblical chronology, to around the time of Adam, Cain, and Abel. The body was carefully examined, and the conclusion drawn was that he died by bleeding to death after being hit in the back by an arrow.

Examiners named the man Otzi. Other artifacts were discovered at the scene, including his stone ax, his shoe of bearskin deer leather and woven grass, an arrowhead dagger, and a Hazelwood and leather quiver and two arrows. The strangest part, in my opinion, is that he had fifty-nine markings on his body, including small crosses on his lower spine, right knee, and both ankle joints. Professor Don Brothwell from the University of York suggests the crosses may have been applied to areas of the body to relieve joint pain. I recall being in Rabbi Yehuda Getz's office shortly after the story of the iceman broke in international news. I saw the cross formations on the ankle and asked the rabbi, "What is the possibility that this emblem was linked to the early Hebrew alphabet and the letter tav, whose emblem was a cross sign?"

He was fascinated by my observation and made a comment to my small group that the plus or the cross emblem was one of the most ancient emblems of protection. He then informed me that, when God placed the mark on Cain's head, it was the form of the letter tav. It would have been a cross or a plus sign, similar to the tattoos on the iceman. We speculated that, since Cain was marked with this sign, his descendants also may have marked themselves with the cross emblem—such as the iceman did over 5,100 years ago.

The Cross is the Universal Sign

In early church days, there is not much evidence that the cross was used as an emblem of Christianity, as it was a very cruel form of punishment that the Romans used on early Christians. In 1969 in Jerusalem, a Greek Monk discovered pottery that had the emblem of the fish and menorah. The menorah represented the Jewish branch of the church, while the fish, called the Ichthys, was used to represent early Christianity. It appears that the fish emblem was an early symbol for Christians. In the fourth century, the Chi-Rho monogram was used and adopted by the Emperor Constantine and became a common emblem for the Christian faith.

By the second century, the cross had become a symbol of Christianity. By the early third century, the early church father Clement of Alexandria used the phrase "the Lord's sign" when speaking of the cross. The early father Tertullian, in his book *De Corona* written in 204 AD, reveals a tradition that existed among the Christians at that time to trace the sign of the cross on their foreheads.

The Christian cross has taken on countless forms since early times. A small list includes:

- Saint Andrew's cross
- Anthony's cross
- Canterbury Cross

- Celtic cross
- Coptic cross
- Greek cross
- Jerusalem's cross
- Latin cross
- Saint Thomas cross

If the sign of Christ is the cross, and His sign will appear in heaven prior to His return to set up the kingdom, then there must be cross symbolism in the heavens.

The Southern Cross

Among the heavenly constellations is one identified as the Southern Cross. Called by its Latin name, Crux, the Southern Cross is the smallest of eighty-eight modern constellations. In ancient times, the cross was visible to the Greeks. In Athens in 1000 BC, it was visible but very low in the sky. By 400 AD, it never again rose above the horizon in Greece.

The Grand Cross

On August 17-18, 1999, all planets except Pluto were either squared or opposite each other. Historically, this marks the end of one cycle and the beginning of another. A weaker version of the Grand Cross appeared on January 11, 1910, the same year that Halley's Comet reappeared. The planets were in a four square position in the heavenly emblems of the lion (Leo) the bull (Taurus) the man (Aquarius) and the eagle (Scorpio).

These four emblems are also the symbols of the four living creatures positioned around the throne of God. These angelic beings have the face of a lion, eagle, ox, and man (Revelation 4:7). These four creatures are also seen when we look at the twelve tribes of Israel as they encamped around the tabernacle. The tribes were divided into four sections of three each—three tribes to the north, three to the south, to the east, and to the west. In each of the four regions, there was one main tribe. Dan was the main tribal family to the north, and Dan's emblem was an eagle. The tribe of Judah camped to the east, and their emblem was a lion. On the south end was Reuben, whose emblem was a man. The emblem of the tribe of Manasseh was an ox, and they settled to the west of the tabernacle.

Oddly enough, these four symbols are also found on the Egyptian sphinx:

- the head is of a man — the emblem of Aquarius
- the front paws are of a lion — the emblem of Leo
- the body and rump are a bull — the emblem of Taurus
- the wings are eagle's wings — the emblem of Scorpio

Several times throughout history, the planets have been positioned to form a Grand Cross in the heavens.

The Whirlpool Galaxy

Thanks to the Hubble Telescope, scientists now know that there are hundreds of billions of galaxies in our universe. A look at the Hubble website will reveal beautiful pictures of these galaxies, with their colorful mixture of gases and stars. One such galaxy is called the Whirlpool Galaxy, which was discovered at the time America was gaining independence from Britain. The galaxy is located within Ursa Major, or the big dipper, which is one of the most recognized constellations. Polaris, or the North Star, is located above the edge of the cup of the big dipper. The North Star has been identified as the brightest star in the heavens and was used as the directional star for ship navigation among the captains of ancient ships. Located at the handle of the dipper is the Whirlpool Galaxy, which is thirty-seven-million light years from earth!

To the naked eye, we see only a blanket of black in the heavens, with small stars that appear as dots blotting the sky. But with the invention and launching of space satellites and the Hubble Telescope, scientists and astronomers were able to look deep into the galaxy and observe secrets that were hidden from men for thousands of years. These great signs have fascinated researchers and awed those who viewed the pictures.

In June of 1992, a series of pictures of the Whirlpool Galaxy were released to the public. One photo in particular revealed an image that was hidden deep in the middle of the galaxy. It was a black hole where space dust and gases were forming a unique shape in the center of the galaxy. In the picture, one can see two "arms" that appear like beams where the hot gases are escaping from the sides of the round, donut-shaped formation. The image is clearly that of a cross!

The Most Important Signs

Most Gentile nations use a Julian calendar that is based upon solar cycles. The Jews use a lunar-solar calendar. However, prophetically, the church does not have a specific calendar. Our future is linked to the fullness of times and the fullness of the Gentiles, as well as to completing our assignment to preach the gospel. For the church, the greatest sign is the gospel being preached "in all the world as a witness unto all nations, and then shall the end come" (Matthew 24:14).

The second sign for the Body of Christ is a universal outpouring of the Holy Spirit that sweeps like a rushing wind into all nations of the world. It will especially impact the sons and daughters, or the younger generation. In Canada, America, and parts of Western Europe, the traditional church consists primarily of individuals over the age of fifty. There is a decline in church attendance, and a lack of interest in both church and Christianity among those of the younger generation. The excuse given is that church is not practical and does not connect to their generation.

Outside of North America and Western Europe, we see a different picture. There is much spiritual activity occurring among the younger generation in Latin America, China, Africa, and even the Islamic nations of the world. In these areas of the world, I am told by missionaries that the Christian church is booming with millions of individuals who are under thirty years of age. Around the world, we are seeing the fulfillment of Joel's prophecy when he wrote that God would pour out His Spirit on all flesh, that sons and daughters will prophesy, and that young men will see visions (Joel 2:28). The Holy Spirit is, indeed, sweeping like a mighty rushing wind into areas of the world that were once closed to the gospel of Jesus Christ.

CHAPTER 8

Great and Fearful Signs From the Second Heaven

The prophetic Scriptures indicate that both great and fearful signs will appear from heaven. This is speaking of the realm of the second heaven, where the sun, moon, and visible stars are positioned. What could occur in the second heaven that would breed such fear in men that their hearts would fail from looking ahead to what is coming? The first thing I think of a large asteroid striking the planet. However, there are other dangerous possibilities that are linked to the sun.

Some scientists are concerned about the sun's activity beginning in the year 2012. The National Academy of Sciences has already outlined a worst-case scenario for 2012. Their theory is based on a solar storm that occurred in 1859, which shortened telegraph wires in both the U.S. and Europe, creating fires in the process. The sun is in an active eleven-year-cycle and, in the year 2012, could release powerful magnetic storms. In the past, this type of sun activity has affected the power grid. A major magnetic storm could disable satellites, disrupt power grids, and shut down communication systems, including cell phones. Since modern power grids are interconnected, this type of solar storm could create an unthinkable disaster for those who depend on power-related technology.

Since everything outside of the third world operates on electricity, including fuel pumps, water distribution plants, food production, refrigeration, and so on, we would feel the impact within the first twelve to twenty-four hours.

In 1989 a sun storm shut down the power in Quebec, Canada. Over a period of two weeks in 2003, ten solar flares knocked out two earth orbiting satellites. According to reports by NASA, the next peak in solar activity is set to occur around 2012. In the past, we saw that some predicted events turned into non-events, and the more this happens, the more likely people will view any future warnings as man crying wolf when there is no wolf. However, the possibility alone should cause a person to make some preparations, in the event that a magnetic storm does occur.

Signs in the Stars

Scientists have discovered a strange cosmic noise that booms six times louder than expected. It emits from a distant cosmos, and nobody is certain what it really is. Sound waves cannot travel in a vacuum, but radio waves can because of their low frequency. The stars, quasars, and the entire Milky Way all emit some form of what is called a "static hiss," first detected by scientists in 1931. This recent discovery was much louder than the static hiss. Alan Kogut said, "Something is going on out there." It is observed that, "Because the radio waves come from far away, traveling at the speed of light, they therefore represent an earlier time in the universe."

Could this cosmic noise be what the writer of Psalm 148 was referring to when he penned the following words?

"Praise ye him, all his angels: praise ye him, all his hosts. Praise ye him, sun and moon: praise him, all ye stars of light. Praise him, ye heavens of heavens, and ye waters that be above the heavens." – Psalm 148:2-4 (KJV)

Scientists also discovered that the earth itself emits a special and unique low humming sound. We know that the worlds were framed by the Word of God (Hebrews 11:3), and that God is upholding His creation by the power of His Word (Hebrews 1:3). Job was informed that, during the creation of heaven and earth, the "sons of God sang together and the morning stars shouted for joy" (Job 38:7). The worlds were created by the spoken words of God, and the spoken word will not pass away (Matthew 24:35). Could these cosmic hums be tangible proof of the creative word of God continuing to circulate throughout the universe? Scientists believe that the universe is continually expanding, and many of them reason that this is proof of progressive evolution. I would suggest that the universe continues to expand because the words that God spoke in the beginning are still active in the universe and cannot be recalled. God is still upholding all things by His Word!

The Possible Meteorite or Asteroid

In the August 2008 issue of National Geographic, Richard Stone wrote an interesting article entitled "Target Earth," in which he discussed the possibility of an asteroid striking the earth. On June 18th, 2004, the Kitt Peak National Observatory spotted an asteroid the size of a sports stadium, and projected a one in forty chance that it could collide with earth. The projection indicates that the asteroid could come within 21,000 miles of earth in 2029, but there is little chance of impact at that point. A scientist suggested that the asteroid could pass through a "key hole", and the earth's gravity could change the asteroid's course when it returns in April of 2036, pulling it into earth's atmosphere. The asteroid was named Apophis, after an Egyptian god of evil and destruction.

The timeframe from 2029 to 2036 is interesting. Many scholars believe that Christ was crucified in April of 32 AD, and the church was born about 50 days later on Pentecost (Acts 2:1-4). From the year 32 AD to the year 2032 is a period of two thousand years. Many early church fathers believed in a two day, or two-thousand-year prophetic cycle, based on Hosea 6:1-2. Second Peter 3:8 says that, one day with the Lord is as a thousand years, and a thousand years is as one day.

Hosea said, "In two days he will revive us…" These two days, according to some, could cryptically refer to two-thousand years, thus indicating the timeframe when the final revival would occur that climaxes in the return of Christ. Let us assume that the asteroid is seen in 32 AD, exactly two thousand years after the crucifixion; then, forty-two months later it returns to strike the earth. This would create the scenario that could make 2032 the date for the return of Christ for the church, and forty-two months later (at mid-tribulation) the asteroid that John saw hitting the earth. While this is not my prediction of coming events, it does create an interesting theory.

The Hadron Collider

All of these natural occurrences are great, and even fearful, signs from the heavens. I believe it is possible, however, that certain unusual prophecies could be fulfilled by inventions of man. For example, researchers have created the Hadron Collider, which is a high energy particle accelerator located in a tunnel beneath the French-Swiss border near Geneva, Switzerland. Scientists are hoping to recreate a "big bang" in their attempt to prove that the universe was formed in this manner.

The machine will send two beams of subatomic particles traveling in opposite directions inside the accelerator, and they will gain speed until they collide head-on at a very high energy level. Scientists hope to create strange new particles that can be studied to prove the big bang theory of evolution. While many are excited about the research and the test, others believe this activity could create a mini black hole that, over time, could destroy the earth:

"Professor Otto Rossler, a German Chemist, is concerned. He said, "My own calculations have shown it is quite plausible that these little black holes survive and will grow exponentially and eat the planet from the inside…"

There are several prophecies in the Bible that indicate a major shaking will occur in the heavenly firmament:

> *"And all the host of heaven shall be dissolved, and the heavens shall be rolled together as a scroll: and all their host shall fall down, as the leaf falls off from the vine, and as a falling fig from the fig tree."*
> —Isaiah 34:4 (KJV)

> *"And the stars of heaven fell unto the earth, even as a fig tree casts her untimely figs, when she is shaken of a mighty wind. And the heaven departed as a scroll when it is rolled together; and every mountain and island were moved out of their places."*
> —Revelation 6:13-14 (KJV)

The general interpretation is that God is sending judgment to the earth by plucking stars from heaven and throwing them to the earth as a manifestation of His wrath. However, Scripture can be seen in a different light when we research the ways that mankind is breaking the limits of creativity to form experiments that may—and I emphasize *may*—alter the molecular structure of both the earth and the heavenly atmosphere. Have we not already done this by splitting the atom and enriching uranium to produce clouds that destroy the land and send deadly radiation into the atmosphere?

Strange Pictures from the Heavens

The Hubble telescope, named after American astronomer Edwin Hubble, was carried into orbit on the space shuttle in April of 1990. The telescope, which takes sharp pictures deep in the cosmic heavens, took an unusual photograph near the time of Passover. The Hubble had photographed NGC-7049, a bright cluster star galaxy in the southern constellation Indus. The photograph revealed a ghostly halo surrounding cosmic dust that clearly appeared as a huge crown of thorns!

Another photograph was released by NASA's Hubble telescope at the Kitt Peak National Observatory in Arizona. The cosmic photograph depicts the Helix-Nebula, a trillion mile long tunnel of glowing gases. In the center is a dying star that is still ejecting masses of dust and gasses. The unusual photo was labeled the "eye of God," as the design of the gases appeared to form a colorful eye in the midst of the nebula.

A third remarkable photograph was captured through the lens of the Hubble telescope. In the midst of the heavens was a comet. The gasses appear to form a large hand, almost appearing to cover the comet.

I would certainly classify these unusual and strange discoveries as great and astonishing signs in the heaven. Cosmic activity is always linked, historically and biblically, to the seasons of redemption.

CHAPTER 8

Preparing for the Final Redemption

One of the final signs of the coming redemption (return of the Messiah) is linked to cosmic activity. As mankind witnesses the signs in the sun, moon, and stars and the great and fearful signs, we are to, "look up and lift up our head, because (our) redemption is drawing near" (Luke 21:28).

In Luke 21 is recorded the order of events that will transpire and lead to the final redemption:

- the destruction of the Jewish Temple — Luke 21:6
- deception in religion — Luke 21:8
- destruction by wars — Luke 21:9
- division in the nations — Luke 21:10
- divers famines, earthquakes, and pestilences — Luke 21:11
- divine signs from heaven — Luke 21:11

In Matthew 24, Mark 13, and Luke 21, strange activity on the sun and moon are indicators of the return of the Messiah to earth. This return is identified by Luke as redemption. In the New Testament, several Greek words are used for redeem and redemption.

In Galatians 3:13, believers were redeemed from the curse of the law. The word redeem here is *exagorazo*, meaning to purchase a slave's freedom, or to buy them out of slavery. This was the first phase of Christ's redemption of mankind; He purchased them out of the slave market of sin. A second word translated redeemed is *lutroo*, and it alludes to the Messiah redeeming Israel. This word refers to a release after receiving the ransom price paid. A third word is *lutrosis*, which describes an act of redemption through the finished work of Christ (Hebrews 9:12). The redemption referred to in Luke 21 that follows the final cosmic signs is the word *apolutrosis*, which identifies the act of Christ delivering His saints when He returns (Luke 21:28). At the Messiah's return, a person will be released from this mortal body of death, and be given a new and immortal body of perfection (1 Corinthians 15:53-54).

Throughout history there have been several major redemptive cycles. The first was when God redeemed His people out of Egyptian bondage:

> *"And who is like Your people Israel, the one nation on the earth whom God went to redeem for Himself as a people—to make for Yourself a name by great and awesome deeds, by driving out nations from before Your people whom You redeemed from Egypt?"*
>
> —1 Chronicles 17:21 (NKJV)

The second great redemption was when God brought Israel back from seventy years of captivity in Babylon:

> *"Be in pain, and labor to bring forth, O daughter of Zion, like a woman in birth pangs. For now you shall go forth from the city, you shall dwell in the field, and to Babylon you shall go. There you shall*

be delivered; there the LORD will redeem you from the hand of your enemies." —Micah 4:10

The third redemption was when Christ, through His atoning work on the cross, brought the possibility of redemption from sin to mankind, for those who would choose to receive His finished work:

"Looking for that blessed hope, and the glorious appearing of the great God and our Savior Jesus Christ; Who gave himself for us, that he might redeem us from all iniquity, and purify unto himself a peculiar people, zealous of good works. —Titus 2:13-14 (KJV)

There is another level of redemption that follows the initial act of being forgiven from sin and redeemed. This is the redemption from destruction. This destruction can be healing from a sickness, deliverance from an addiction, or prevention of premature death by Divine intervention.

"Bless the LORD, O my soul, and forget not all his benefits: who forgiveth all thine iniquities; who healeth all thy diseases; who redeemeth thy life from destruction; who crowneth thee with lovingkindness and tender mercies." —Psalm 103:2-4 (KJV)

"He has sent redemption to His people; He has commanded His covenant forever: Holy and awesome is His name."
—Psalm 111:9

The redemption that believers are anticipating in the future is the redemption that Luke spoke of. This redemption is a part of our new spiritual nature that eagerly anticipates the moment that the final redemption will occur:

> *"Not only that, but we also who have the first fruits of the Spirit, even we ourselves groan within ourselves, eagerly waiting for the adoption, the redemption of our body."* — Romans 8:23

Understanding Redemptive Cycles

Throughout history, redemption is preceded by travail. This travail represents birth pains mentioned throughout the Scriptures. The day of the Lord initiates travail (Isaiah 13:8), just as the rebirth of modern Israel as a nation occurred after the holocaust, a seven-year season of Israel's worst travail. Isaiah 66:8 states that, "When Zion travails, she shall bring forth children." In Matthew 24, Christ warned that wars, famine, earthquakes, and pestilence would be the beginning of sorrows. This English word sorrows is actually the Greek word *odin*, which refers to sorrow, travail, or birth pangs. In every redemptive cycle there are birth pangs.

Another interesting point is that, during major redemptive cycles, children are assaulted, abused, and slain. I believe this is because the adversary is attempting to either remove the future seed, or keep it from maturing and rising to power and thus defeating the plans of the enemy. Premature death of innocent children forever silences the potential voice of these future leaders.

Before Israel's departure from Egypt, the sons of the Hebrews were to be killed immediately after their birth (Exodus 1:15-21). Prior to the Jews being spared from the evil Haman, there was a threat to slay all

Jews in one-hundred-twenty provinces (book of Esther). At the time of Christ's birth, Herod ordered that the infants two years and under be slain in Bethlehem and the area of Rama (Matthew 2:18). Prior to the reformation of modern Israel, the Nazi hordes slew six million Jews, including 1.5 million children. Historically, before a major redemptive cycle, attacks are initiated against the children and innocents.

During each redemptive cycle, the Almighty also raises up a messenger with a voice that is respected and heard among the common people. In Egypt it was Moses; in Persia it was Esther. In Christ's day, it was John the Baptist. In today's society, we have given the voice to politicians and leaders who have become compromisers of truth. However, as we enter a redemptive cycle, the voice of the remnant will turn from an echo in the wilderness to a voice of authority in the mainstream.

Every historical and Biblical redemptive cycle is connected to a set time period. When the time arrives for the cycle to be fulfilled, that period of time is identified in Scripture as the "fullness of time." God promised that Israel would be freed from Egyptian slavery after four hundred years (Genesis 15:13). The Hebrew nation was informed that, after seventy years in Babylonian captivity (Jeremiah 25:11), the nation would be released to return to Israel and rebuild Jerusalem and the Temple. Christ was given a period of about thirty-three years to live and minister before the redemption of mankind was complete. Even the future tribulation has a set time of seven years (Daniel 9:27), divided in two parts of forty-two months each (Revelation 11:2 and 13:5).

According to Paul in Galatians 4:4, Christ was born during the fullness of time. This fullness of time is found in Daniel chapter 9 when the prophet reveals a four-hundred-year prophetic cycle that will impact

Israel. He gives an amazing prediction that, from the decree to rebuild Jerusalem to the time the Messiah is "cut off," will be a total of 483 years (see a detailed explanation in Daniel chapter 9). Scholars have noted that, from the time the decree was given to rebuild the city, to the time of the crucifixion of Christ, is a 483-year period. When prophetic time cycles run full circle and the fullness of time is complete, there is major transition and change that follows and disrupts life as people normally know it.

Another unique pattern of redemption cycles is seen in the way that certain events occur during each cycle. If we look at the Egyptian cycle, the crucifixion cycle, and the final redemption brought by the Messiah's return, we see seven things that occurred during these cycles.

First, let's look at the redemption from Egypt. They experienced:

- Cosmic activity — darkness over the land of Egypt (Exodus 10:22)
- Slavery/bondage — the people were in bondage (Exodus 1:14)
- Killing infants — midwives told to drown the Jewish boys (Exodus 1:16)
- A deliverer arose — Moses was sent to free the people (Exodus 3)
- Healing was manifested — People were healed by eating the lamb (Psalm 105:37)

- Visions and Dreams — God appeared to Moses in a burning Bush (Exodus 3:2-4)
- Judgment came — Egypt saw ten plagues and the destruction of Pharaoh's army (Exodus 6-13)

As God was preparing for the redemption of mankind through Christ, notice that the same seven events transpired:

- Cosmic activity — the Magi saw a star/darkness over Jerusalem at the crucifixion
- Slavery/bondage — Israel was occupied by the Roman soldiers (Matthew 27)
- Killing infants — Herod killed children under two years of age near Bethlehem (Matthew 2:16)
- A deliverer arose — Christ delivered us from sin (Colossians 1:13)
- Healing manifested — Christ's blood brought healing through His stripes (1 Peter 2:24)
- Visions and Dreams — The wise men, Joseph, and others had dreams (Matthew 1:20 and 2:12)

- Judgment came   – Within one generation Jerusalem was destroyed Matthew 24:34)

It is interesting to see how the third redemption—the anticipated return of Christ—has the same signs of the previous two redemptions. We are seeing great and fearful cosmic signs. There is an increase in seducing spirits and doctrines of devils holding multitudes in chains of spiritual bondage and addiction (1 Timothy 4:1). Both Pharaoh and Herod considered it acceptable to kill infants. America alone has slain nearly fifty-million innocent infants through the violent act of abortion since 1973. The deliverer that God has raised up is the remnant church that continues to proclaim the delivering message of the gospel. There is a fresh revelation of healing through receiving the Lord's Supper that is sweeping the church. I also believe we will see instant and miraculous healings in the months and years ahead. The prophetic Scriptures indicate that God will pour out His Spirit upon sons and daughters, and that there will be an increase in dreams and visions (Joel 2:28-29; Acts 2:17). These six parallel signs are indicators that the seventh sign will be witnessed—the decline and destruction of the Gentile nations at the time of the end.

High Anticipation

There is always a sense of high anticipation prior to an important, prophetic redemption cycle. This is pointed out when Mary and Joseph brought the eight-day-old infant Christ child to the Holy Temple to have Him circumcised. Two older believers were present in the Temple compound—a rabbi and a prophetess. The book of Luke records:

> "And behold, there was a man in Jerusalem whose name was Simeon, and this man was just and devout, waiting for the Consolation of Israel, and the Holy Spirit was upon him. And it had been revealed to him by the Holy Spirit that he would not see death before he had seen the Lord's Christ." —Luke 2:25-27

> "Now there was one, Anna, a prophetess, the daughter of Phanuel, of the tribe of Asher. She was of a great age, and had lived with a husband seven years from her virginity; and this woman was a widow of about eighty-four years, who did not depart from the temple, but served God with fastings and prayers night and day. And coming in that instant she gave thanks to the Lord, and spoke of Him to all those who looked for redemption in Jerusalem." —Luke 2:36:38 (NKJV)

I believe that Rabbi Simeon was aware of Daniel's prediction of the *timing* of the Messiah and was in high anticipation of the redeemer's arrival. When Simeon saw Christ, the Almighty impressed upon him that he was viewing the Messiah. The same was true with the eighty-four-year-old Anna. Just as the old rabbi was promised not to die until he saw the Messiah, there is a generation that will not pass through physical death before they see the appearing of Christ in the clouds of glory!

Cosmic Signs in the Final Generation

In three of the four gospels, notice the order of events following the strange cosmic signs in the heaven:

> "Immediately after the tribulation of those days shall the sun be darkened, and the moon shall not give her light, and the stars shall fall from heaven, and the powers of the heavens shall be shaken: And then shall appear the sign of the Son of man in heaven: and then shall all the tribes of the earth mourn, and they shall see the Son of man coming in the clouds of heaven with power and great glory."
> —Matthew 24:29-30 (KJV)

> "But in those days, after that tribulation, the sun shall be darkened, and the moon shall not give her light, and the stars of heaven shall fall, and the powers that are in heaven shall be shaken. And then shall they see the Son of man coming in the clouds with great power and glory."
> —Mark 13:24-26 (KJV)

> "And there shall be signs in the sun, and in the moon, and in the stars; and upon the earth distress of nations, with perplexity; the sea and the waves roaring; men's hearts failing them for fear, and for looking after those things which are coming on the earth: for the powers of heaven shall be shaken. And then shall they see the Son of man coming in a cloud with power and great glory.
> —Luke 21:25-27 (KJV)

All three gospel writers mention how that, one of the final important events that will precede the visible return of Christ to earth to rule and reign in His millennial kingdom, are cosmic signs in the sun, moon, and stars. In light of this, there has never been a generation that can view the wonders of the heavenly firmament and bring dream-like images back to earth as we can today. There has never been a generation that can study the heavens and the sun, moon, and stars in such detail as we can in this generation.

Cosmic activity has preceded all previous seasons of redemption, and strange cosmic activity will again become a central feature prior to the final redemption. It appears that many of these signs in the heavens could begin in the year 2012 and continue from time-to-time for many years, culminating in the return of Jesus Christ to rule and reign on earth for a thousand years.

The heavens are sending us a message that the signs of the times are upon us, and that the end of the age is rapidly approaching. As we watch for the signs of our Messiah's return, let us keep in mind some things He told us. Matthew 24:14 records that Jesus said, *"This Gospel of the kingdom will be preached in all the world as a witness to all the nations, and then the end will come."* The message of the Gospel must be spread around the world to every tribe, tongue, and nation before the return of Christ.

He said that we should watch, because nobody knows the day nor the hour of His coming. Matthew 24:44 records His words, *"Therefore you also be ready, for the Son of Man is coming at an hour you do not expect."*

Finally, Luke 21:34-36 tells us, *"But take heed to yourselves, lest your hearts be weighed down with carousing (self-indulgence), drunkenness, and cares of this life, and that Day come on you unexpectedly. For it will come as a snare (a trap) on all those who dwell on the face of the whole earth. Watch therefore, and pray always that you may be counted worthy to escape all these things that will come to pass, and to stand before the Son of Man."*

We can and should watch for and understand the signs that point to the return of Christ to catch away His spotless bride; but if you are not spiritually prepared for His return, the endeavor is pointless. As you watch and wait for Christ's return, it is important to be ready when the trumpet sounds. Then you can rest assured that, when you see these things begin to happen, you can look up and lift up your head, because your redemption is drawing near!